Cayucos

collected images

Being colorblind gives an advantage when composing black & white... less confusion.

This special collection exhibits the lonely freedom of a hidden perspective. All images presented genuine without edits. Color sacrificed through a unique process.

info@ BEACHNOISE.com

JH Fleming

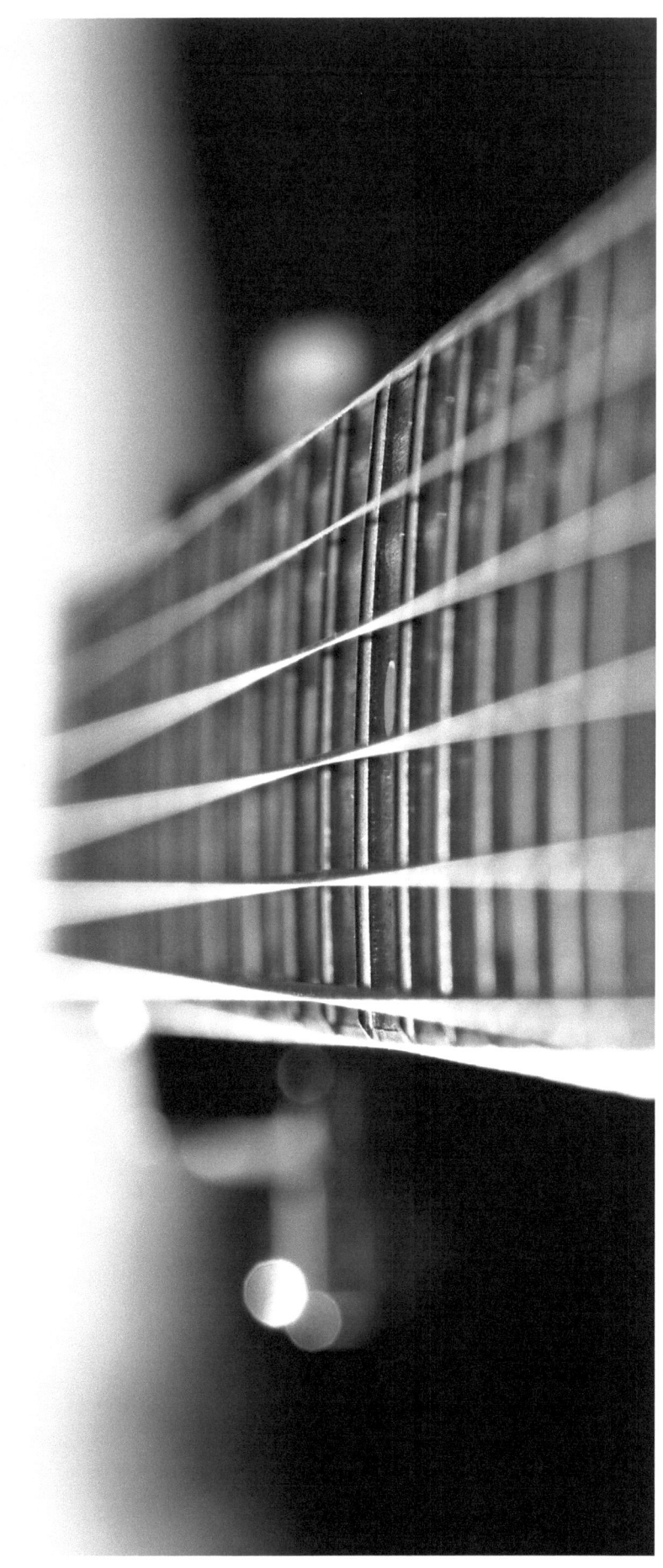

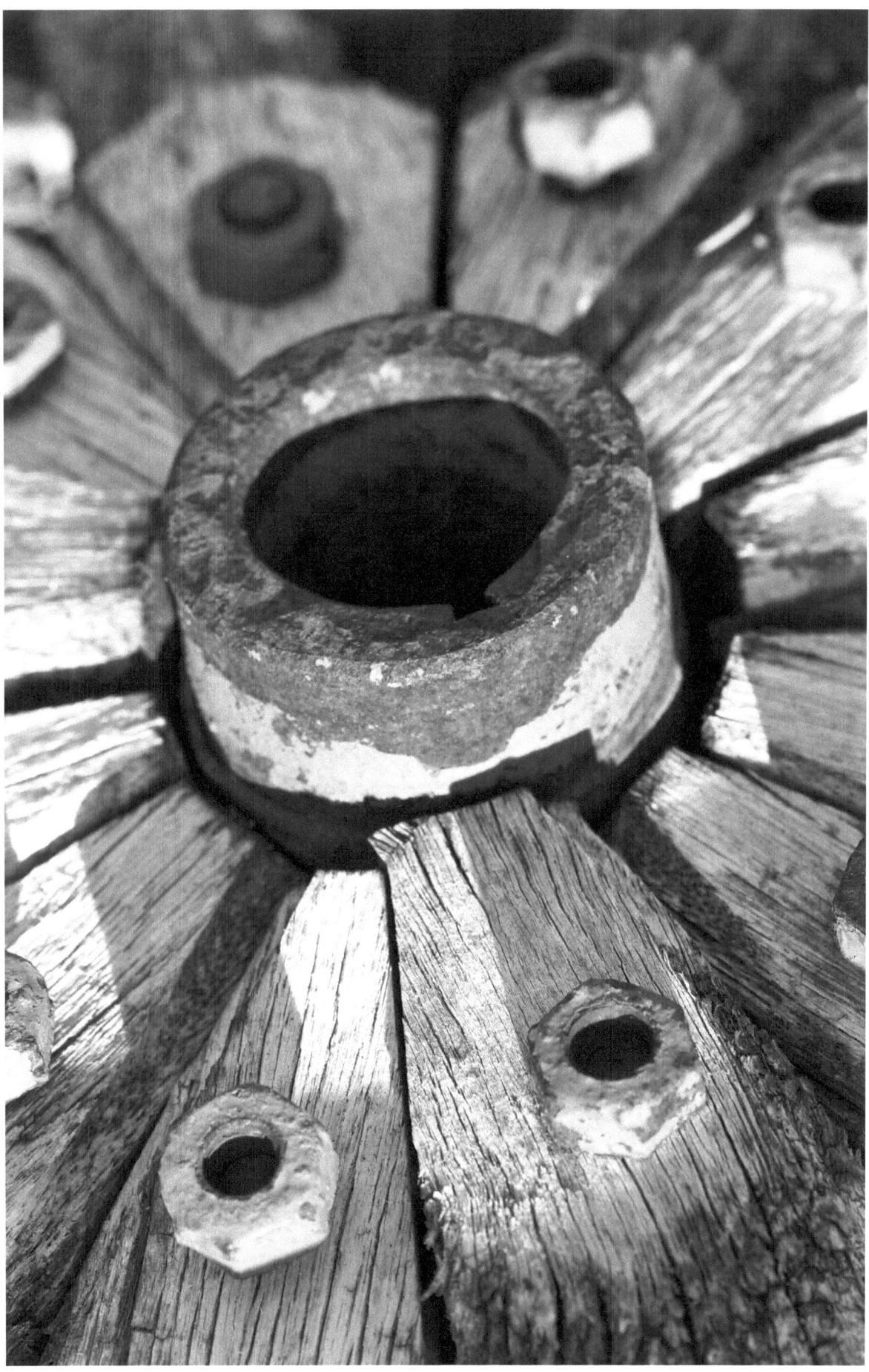

0705

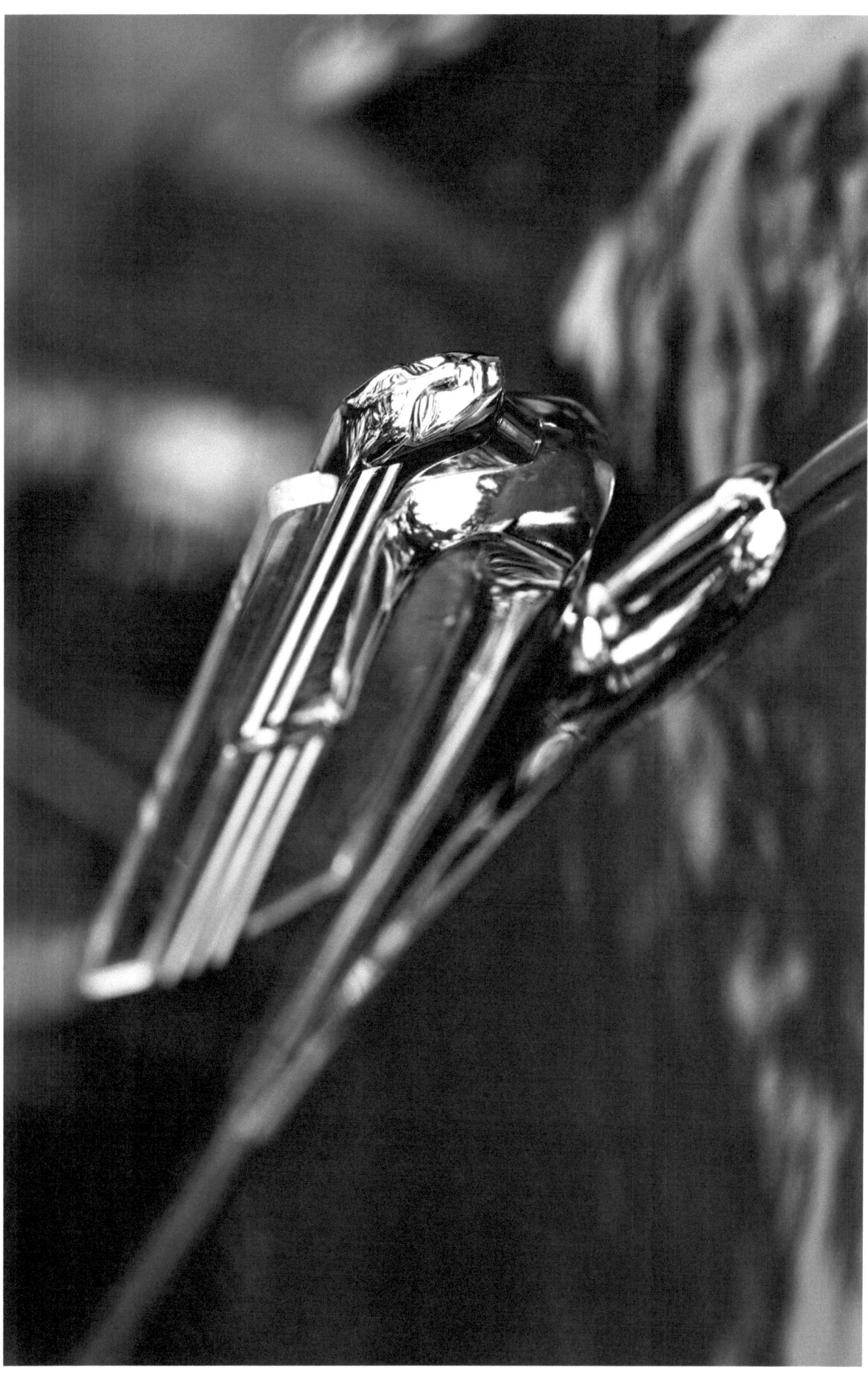

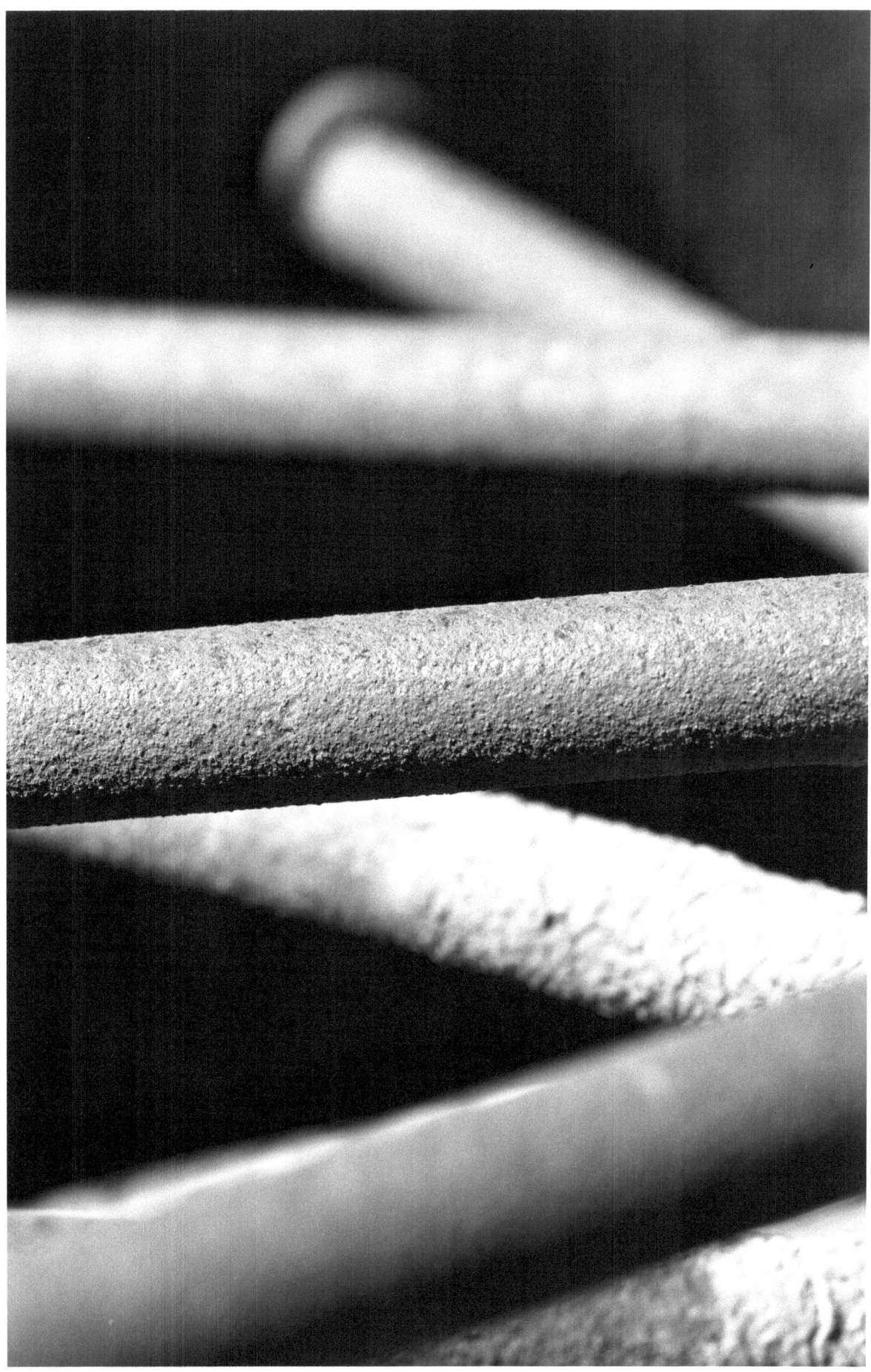

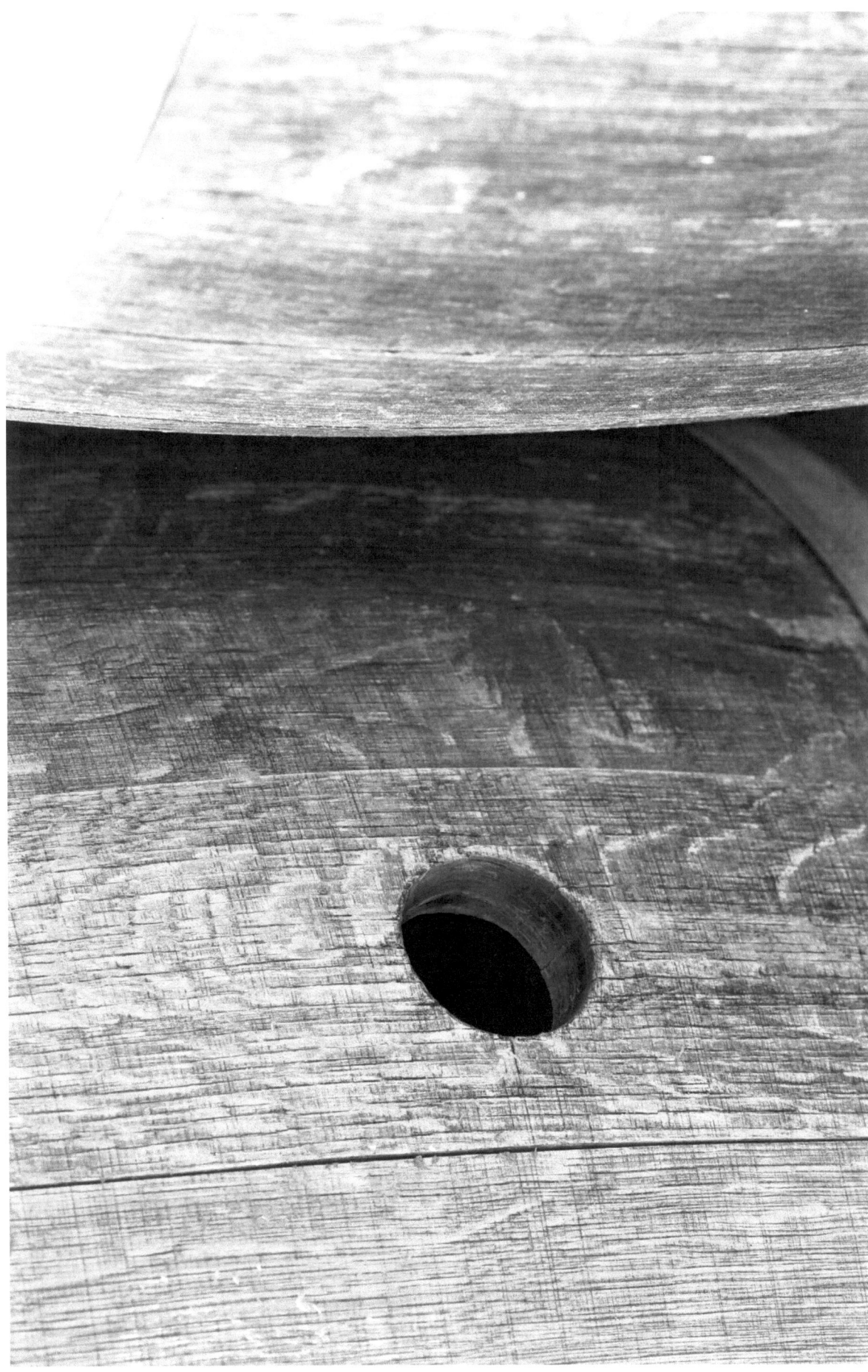

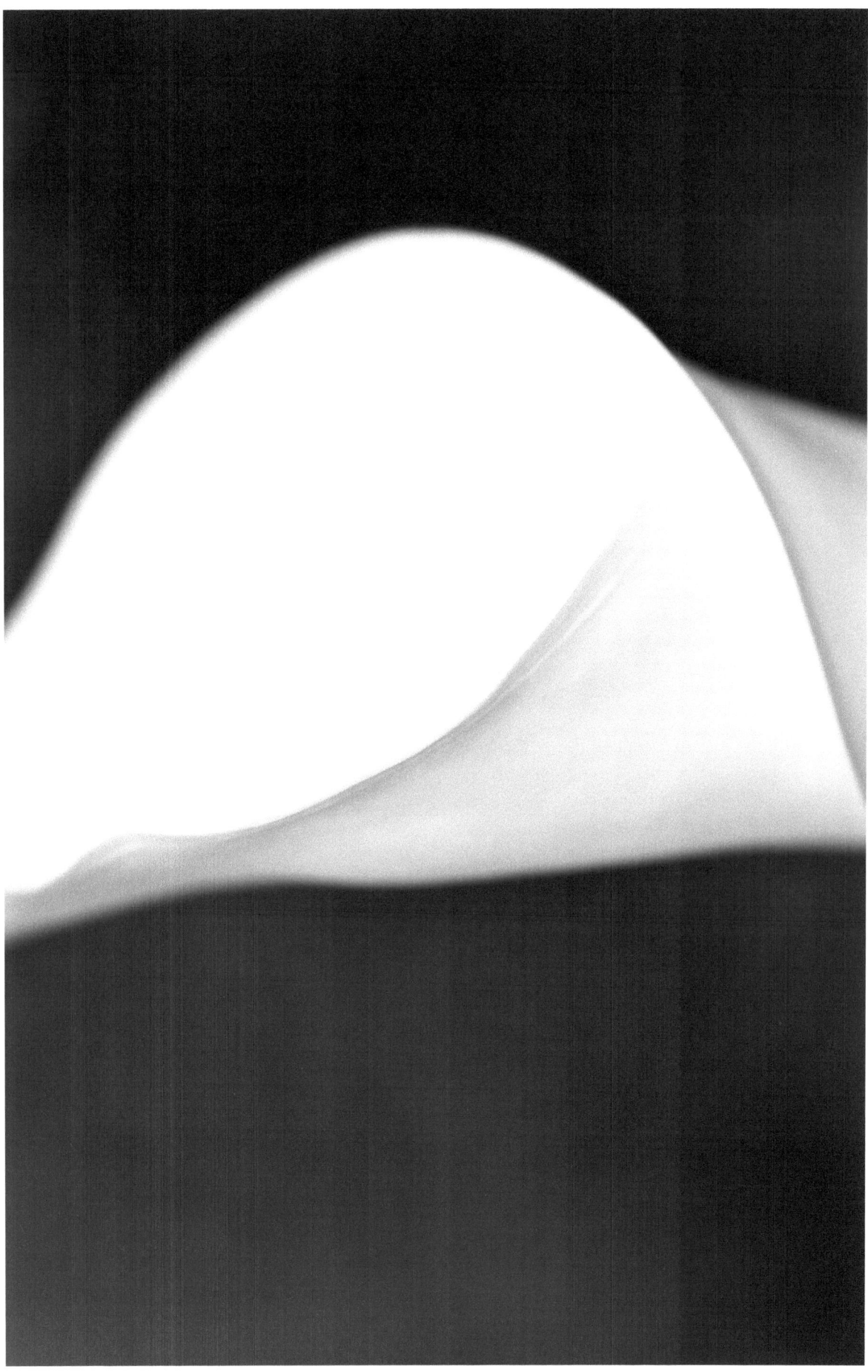

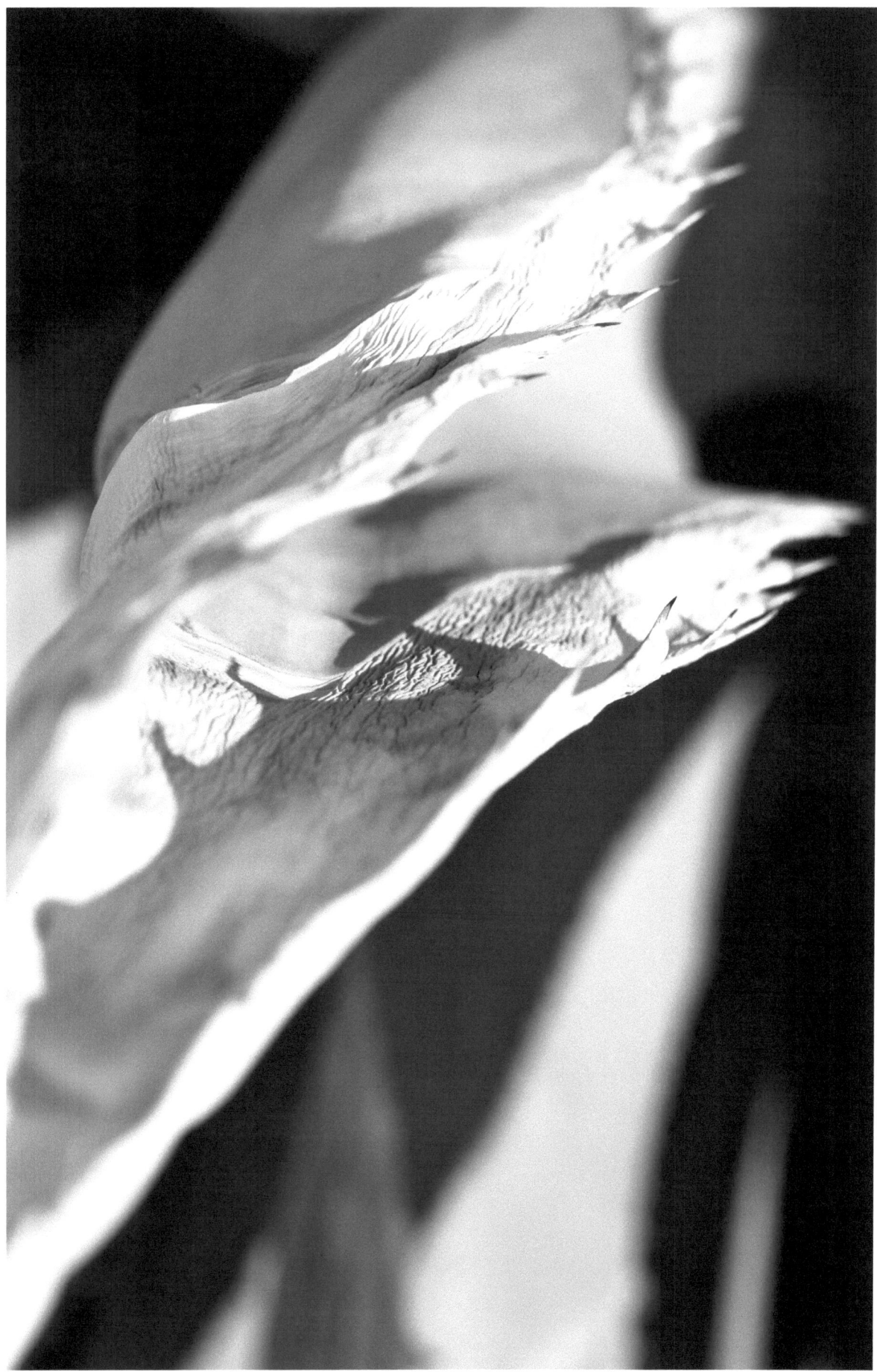

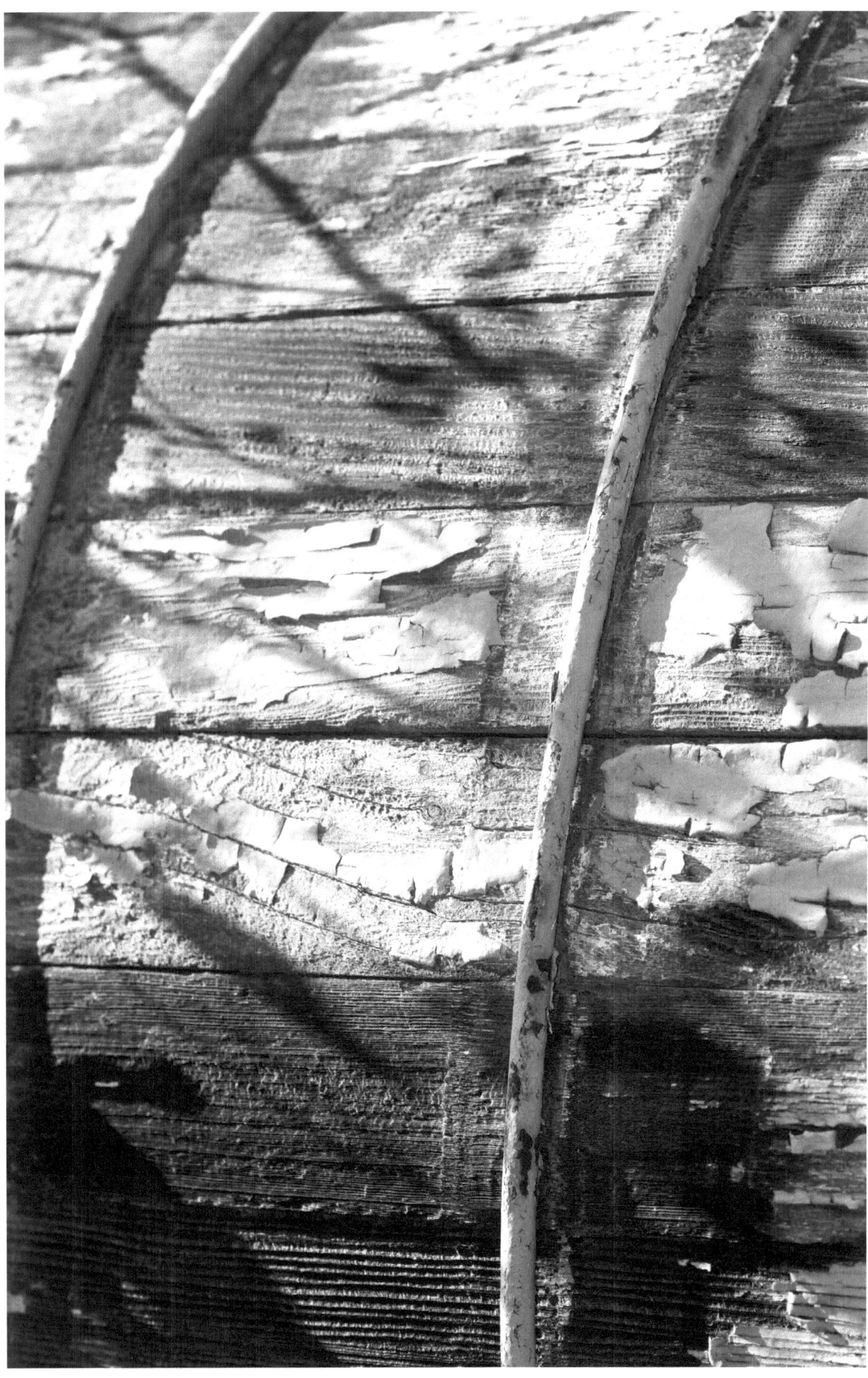

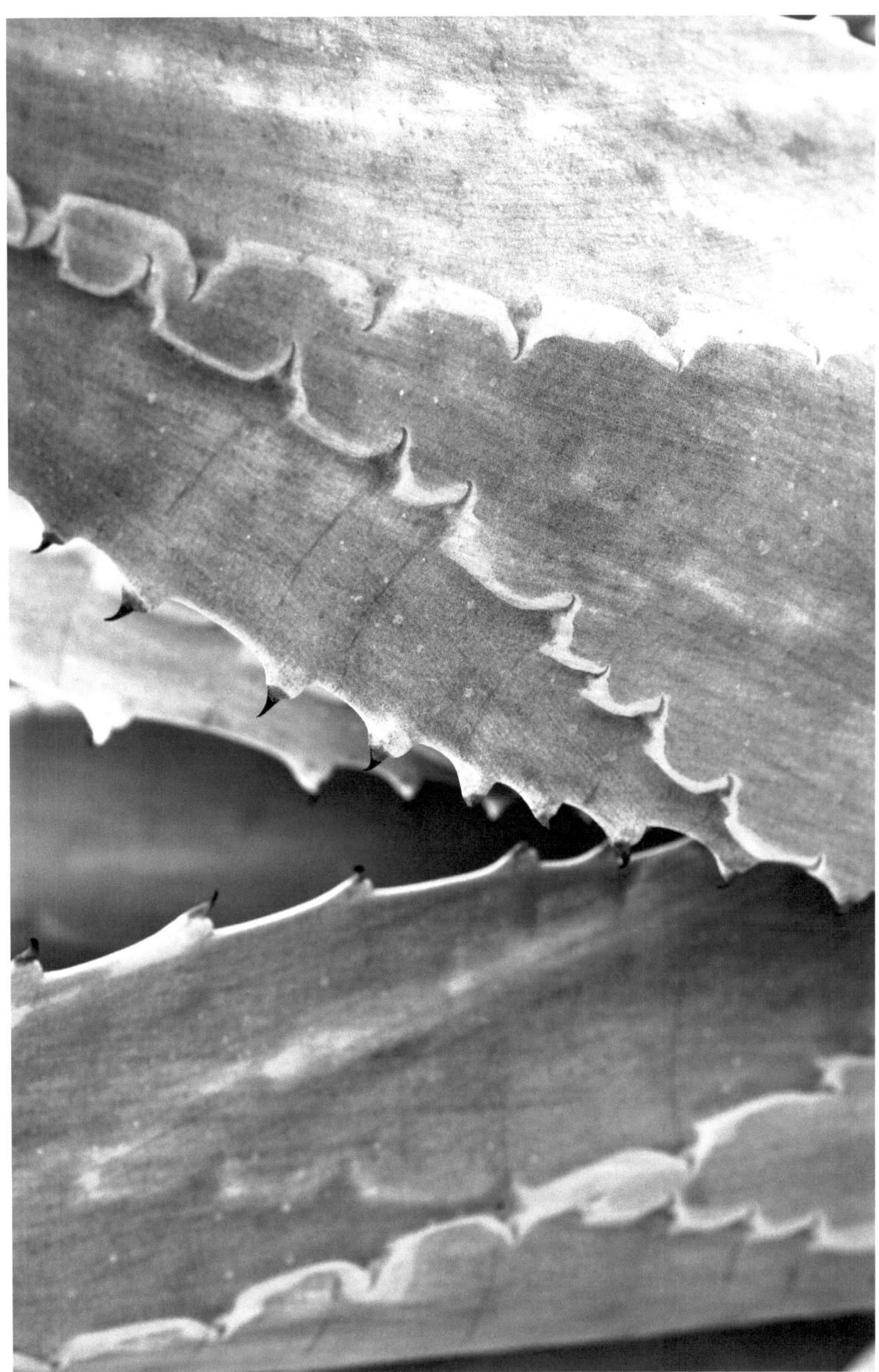

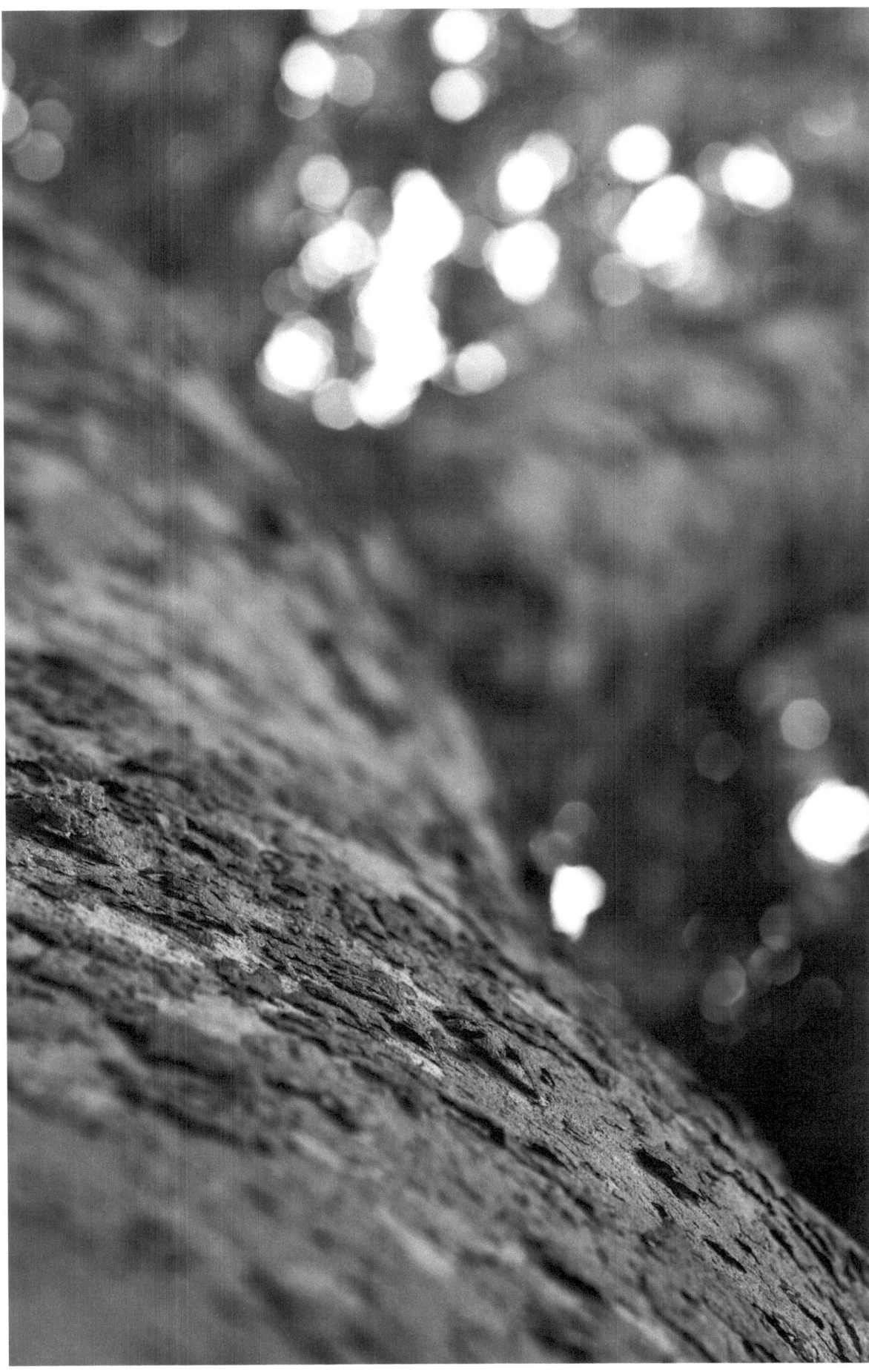

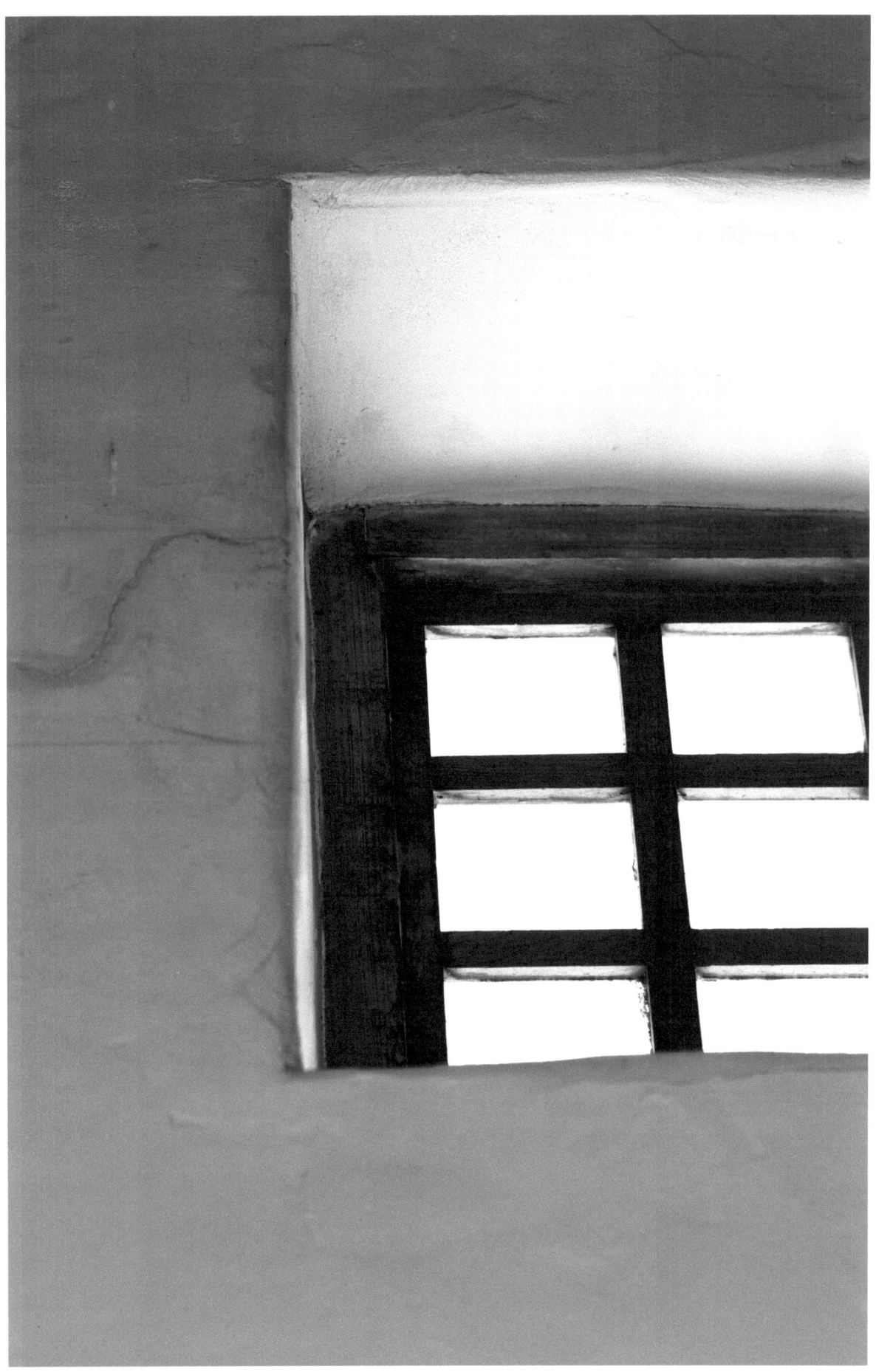

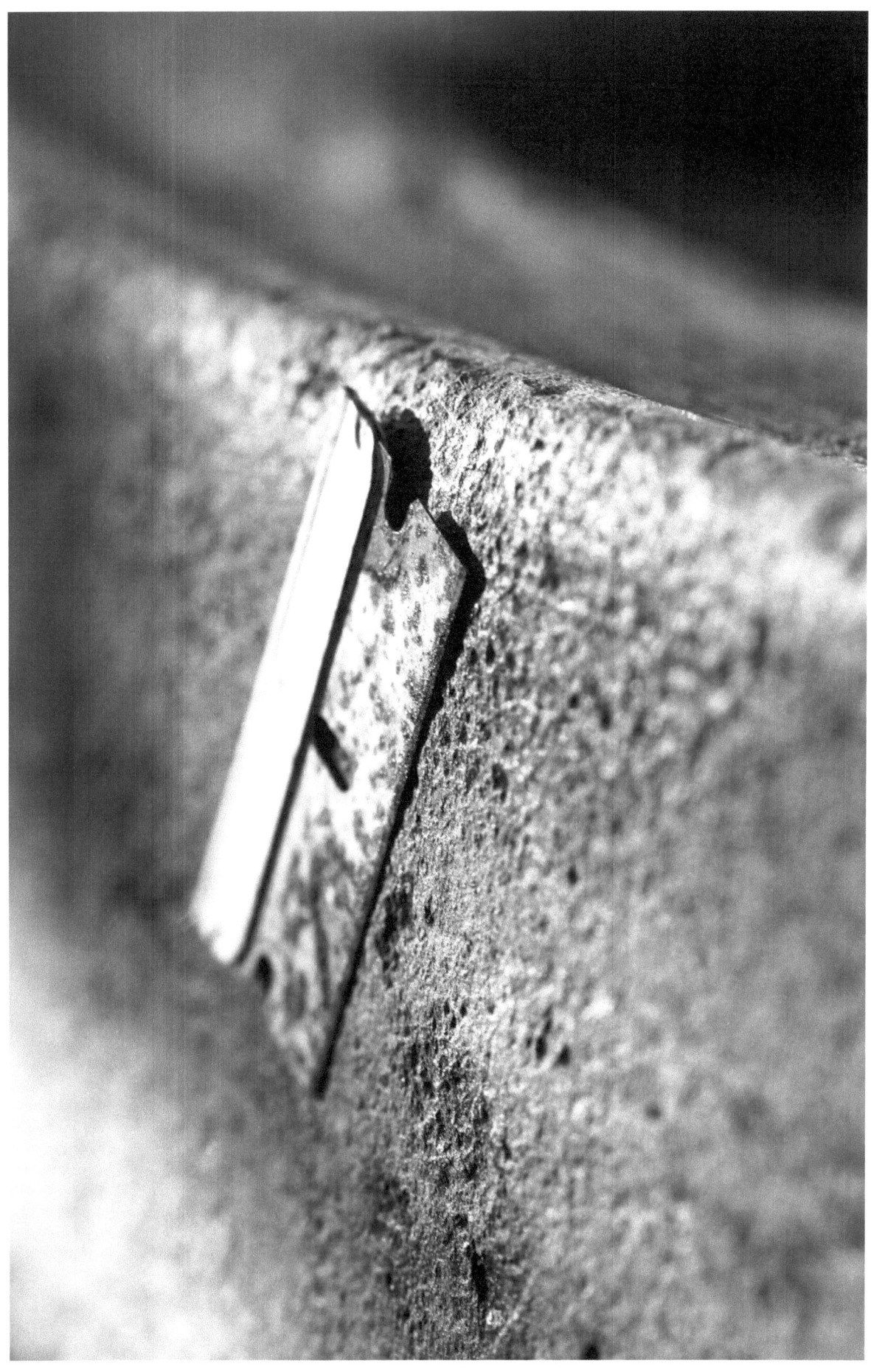

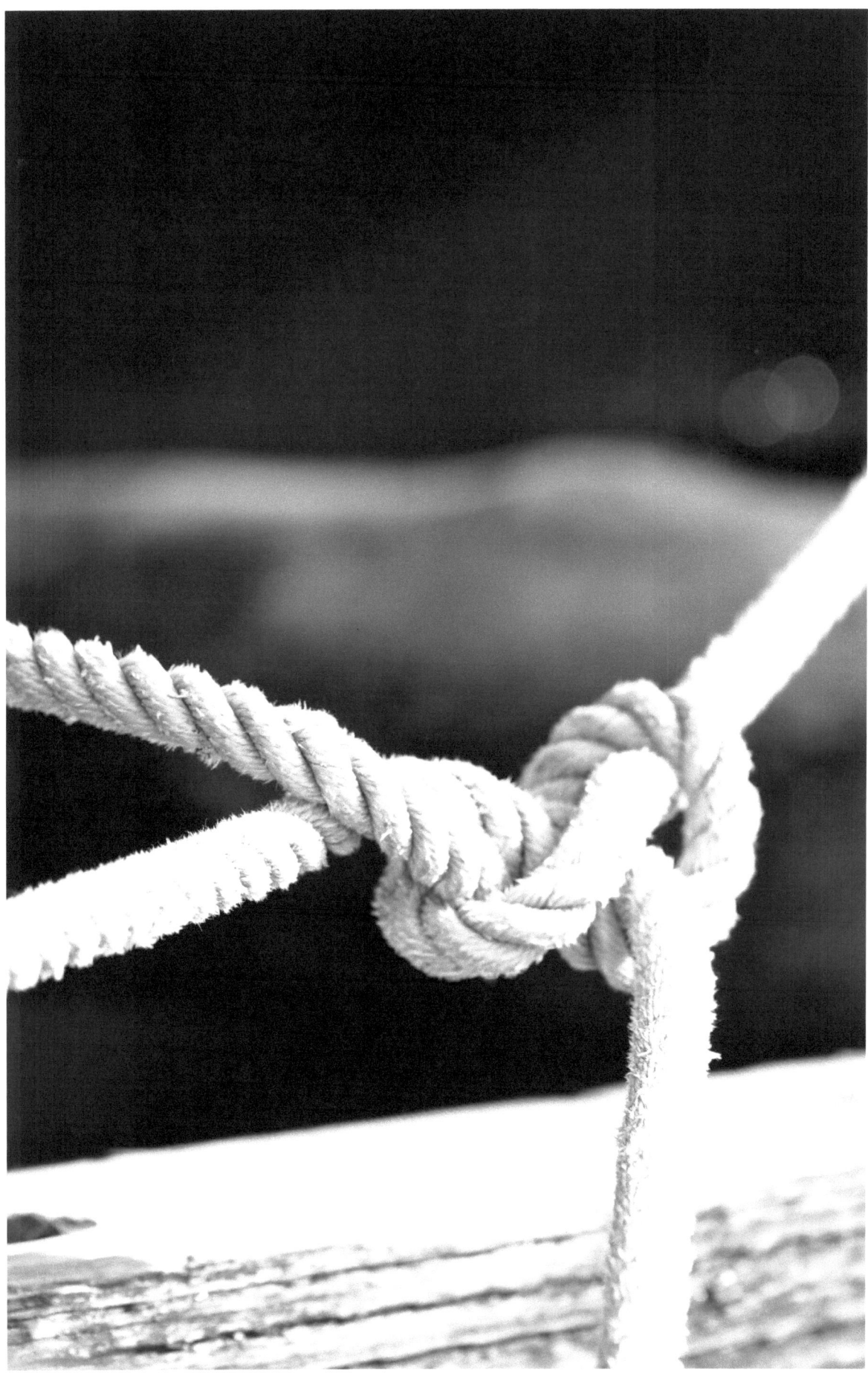

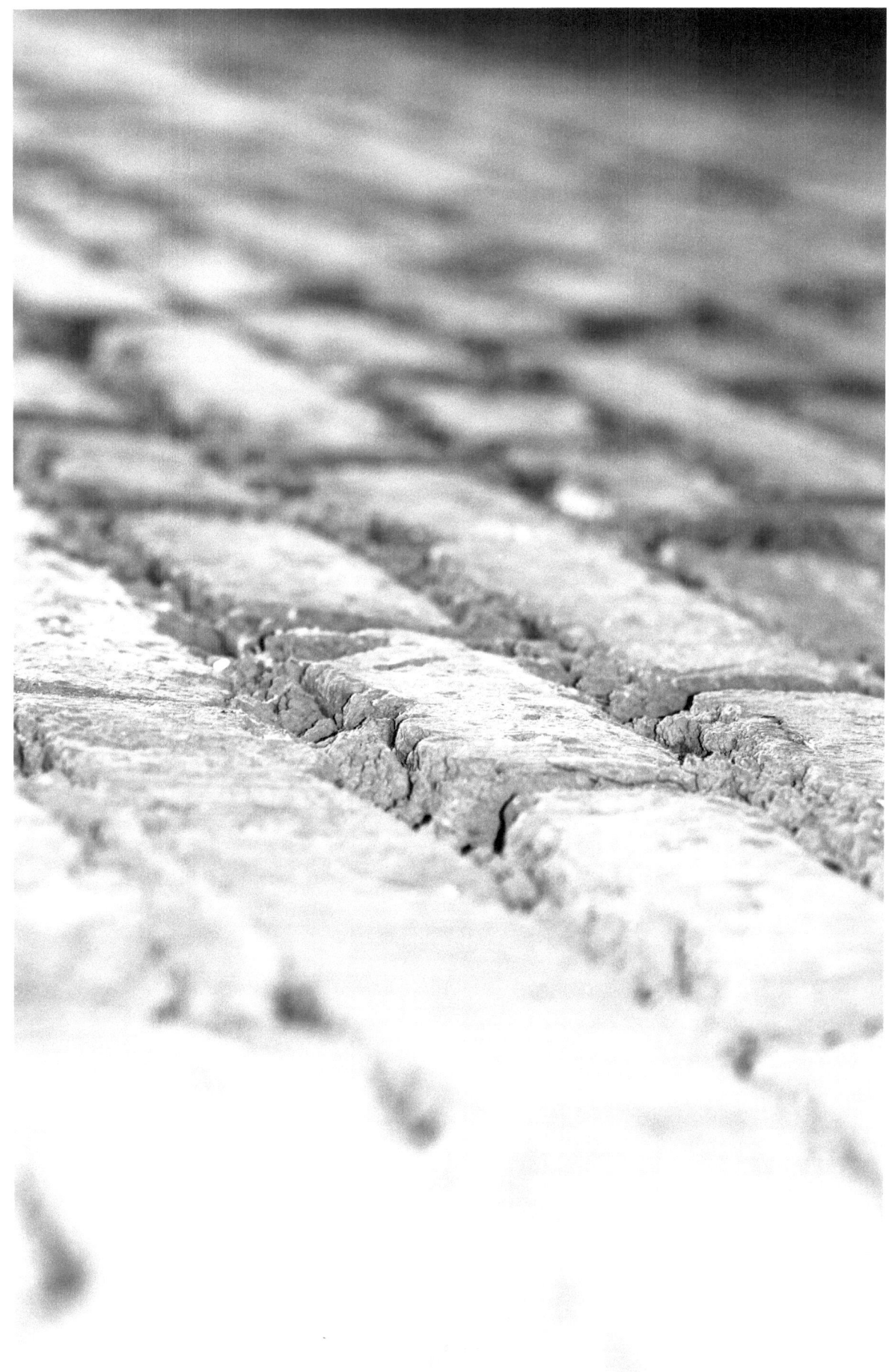

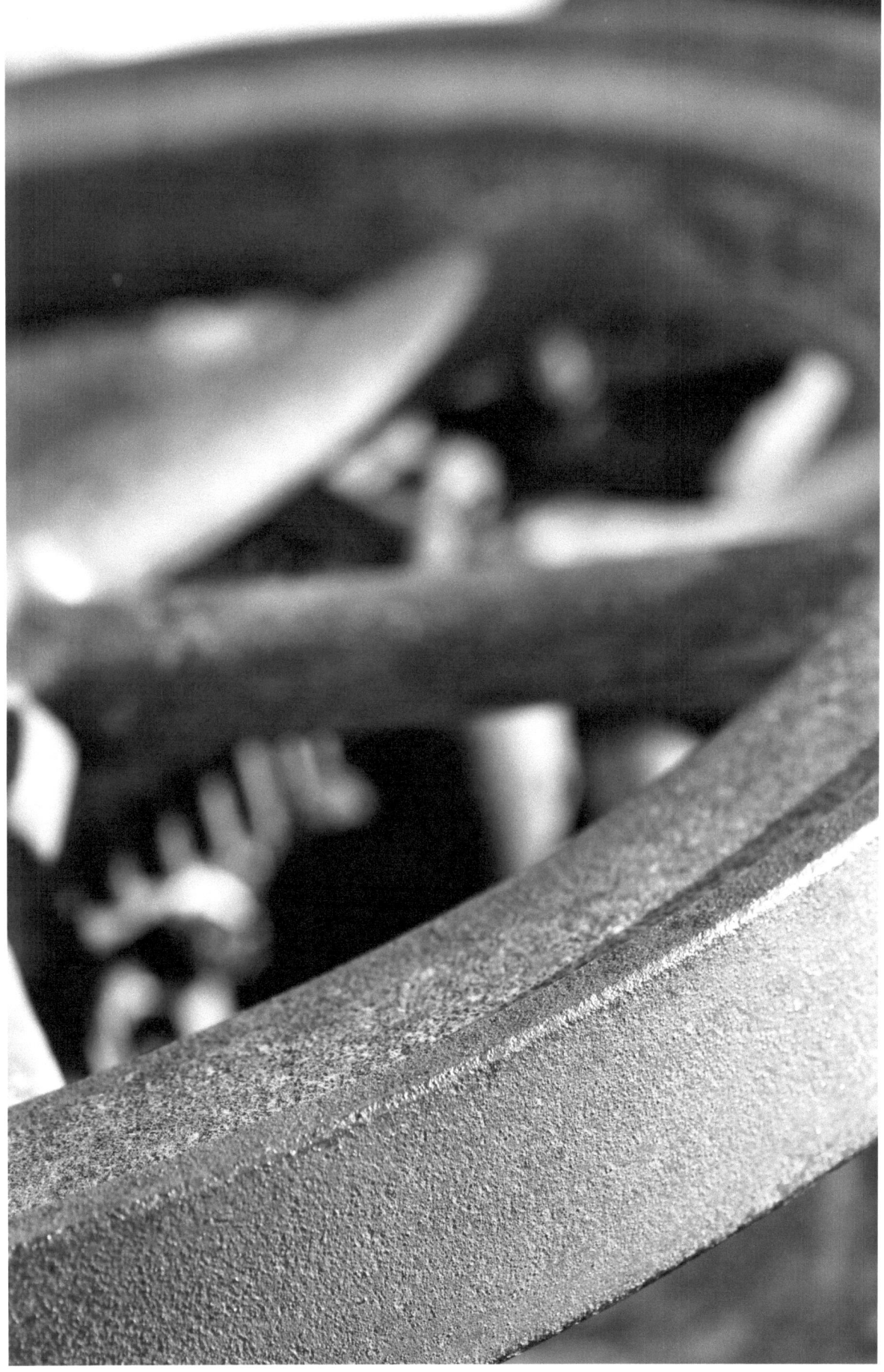

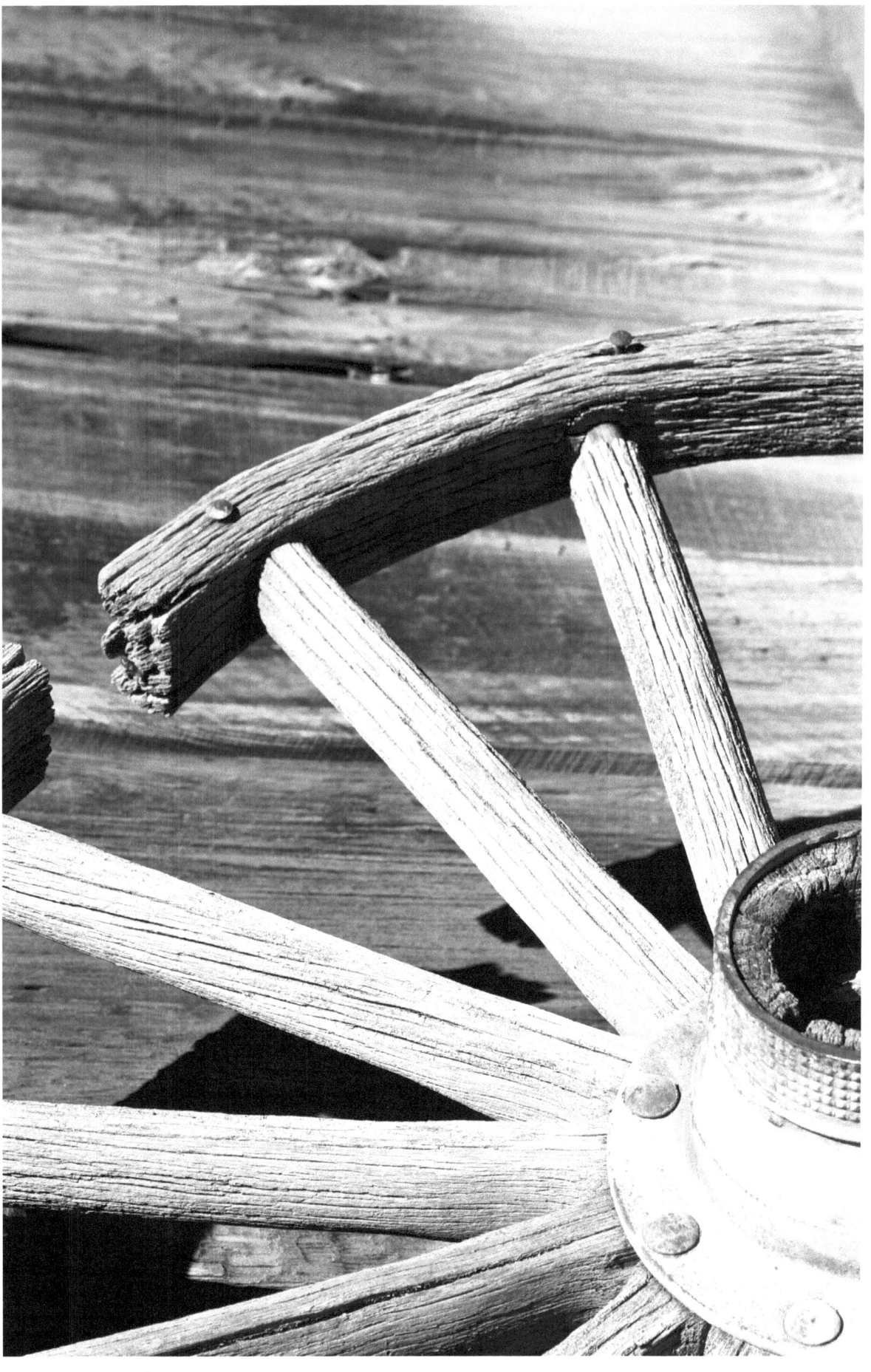

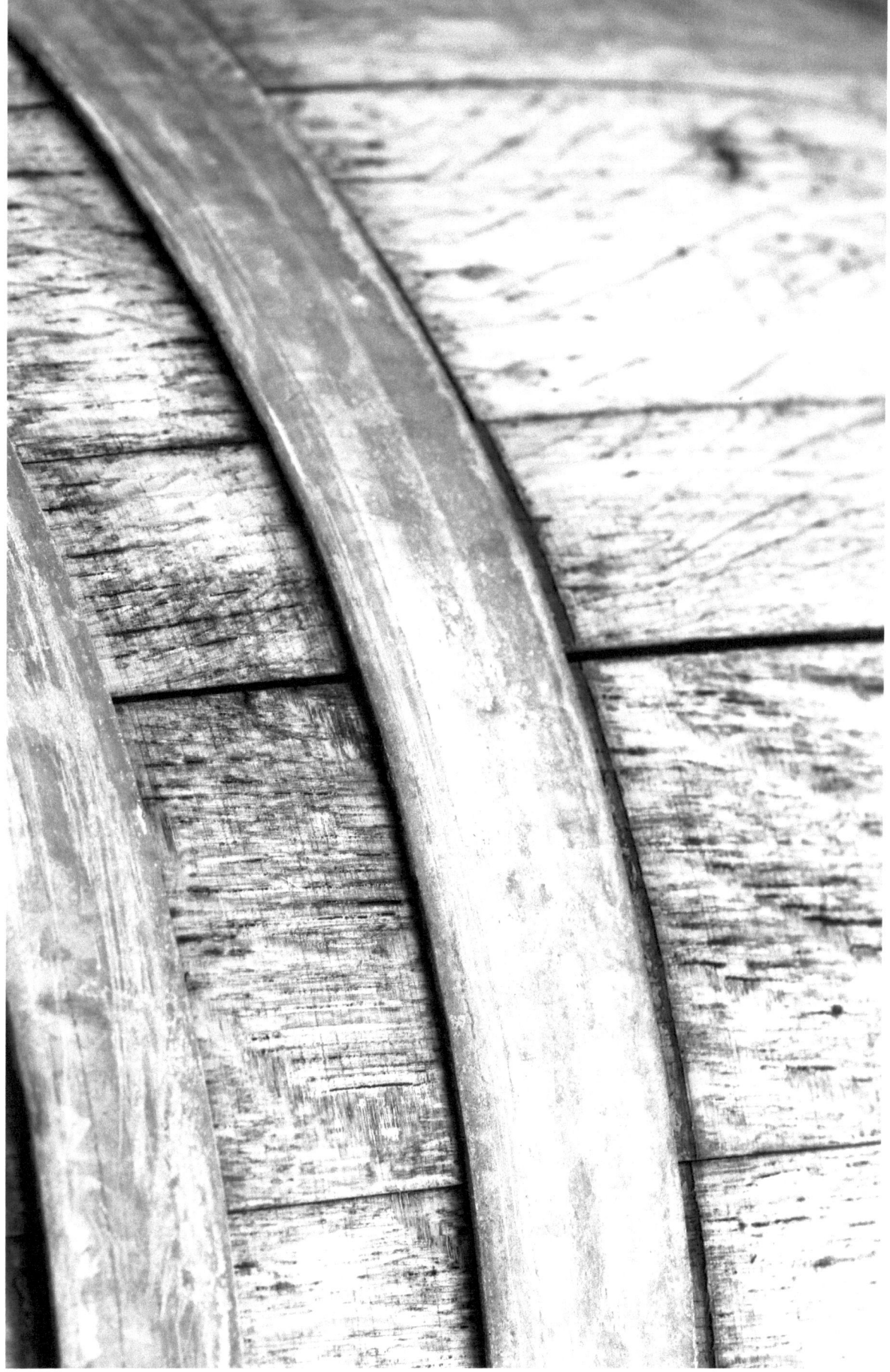

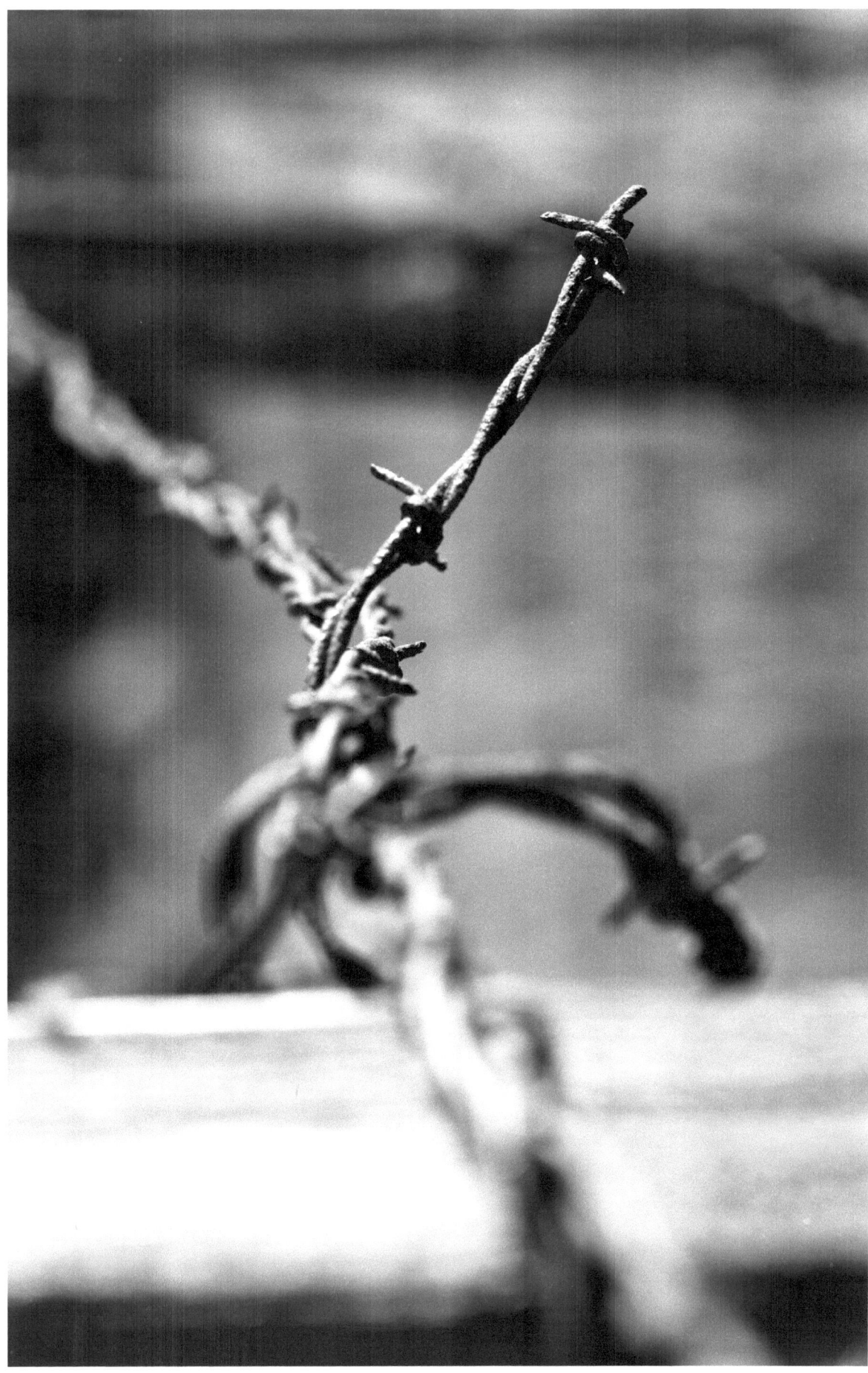

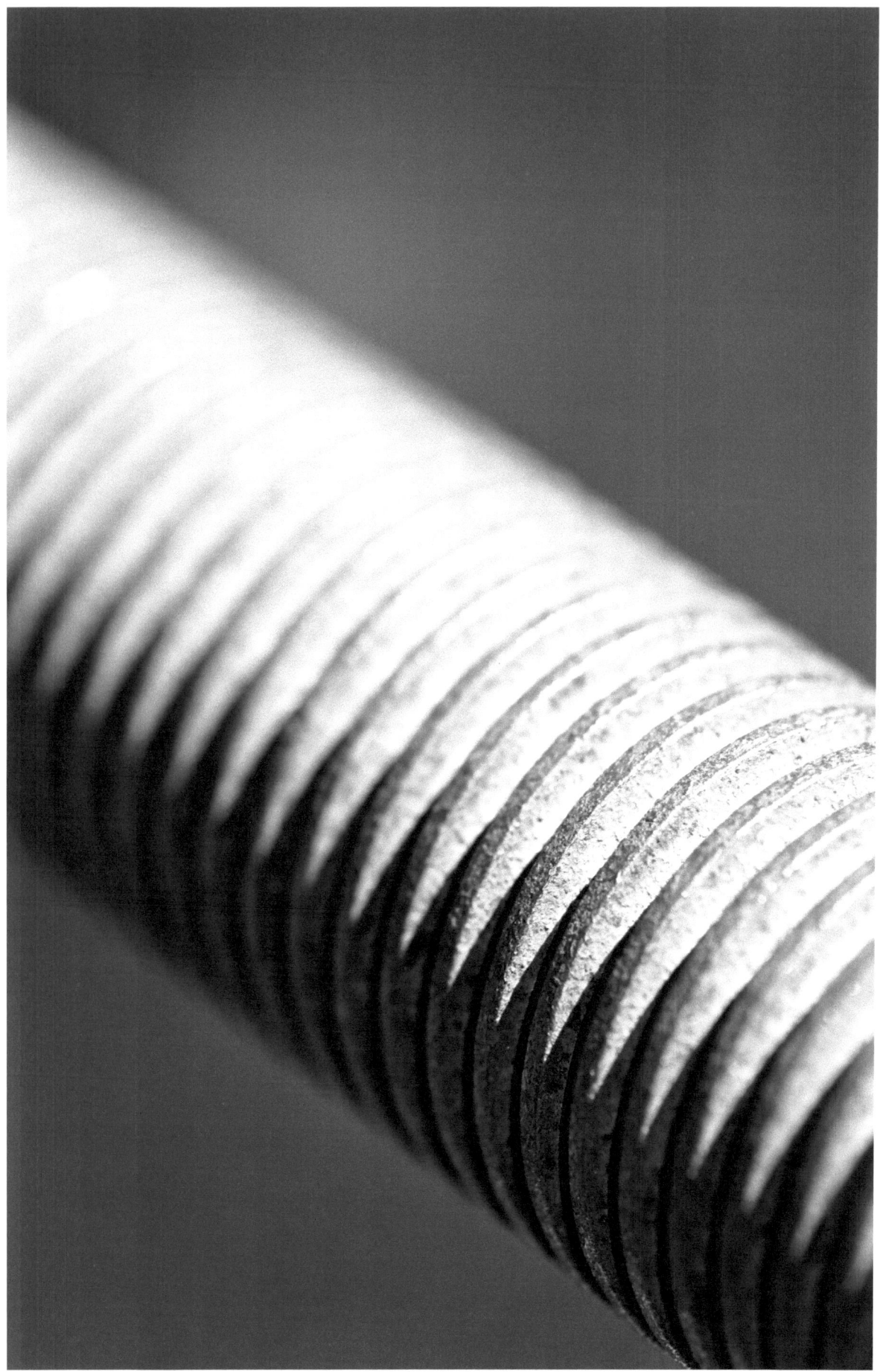

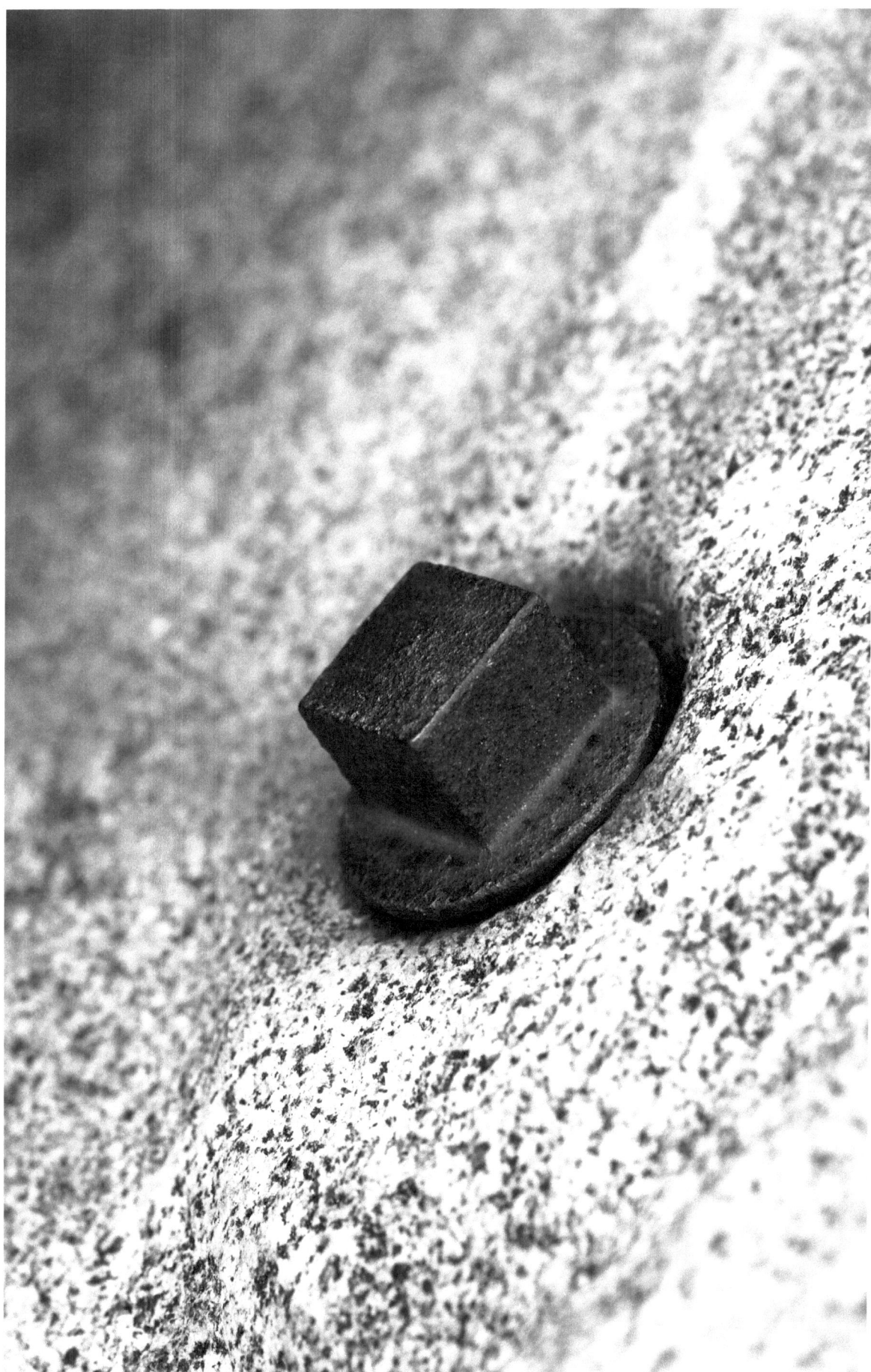

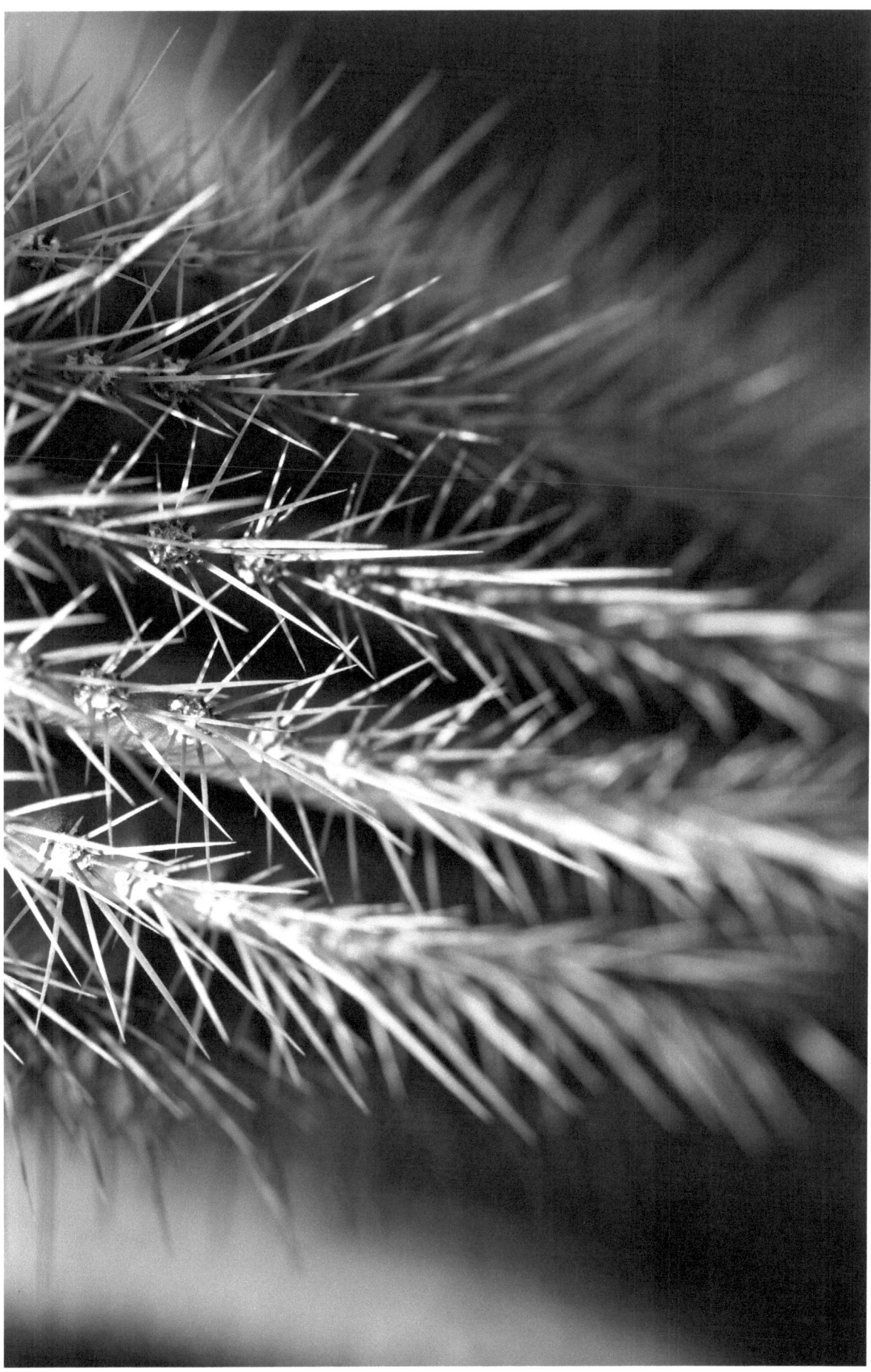

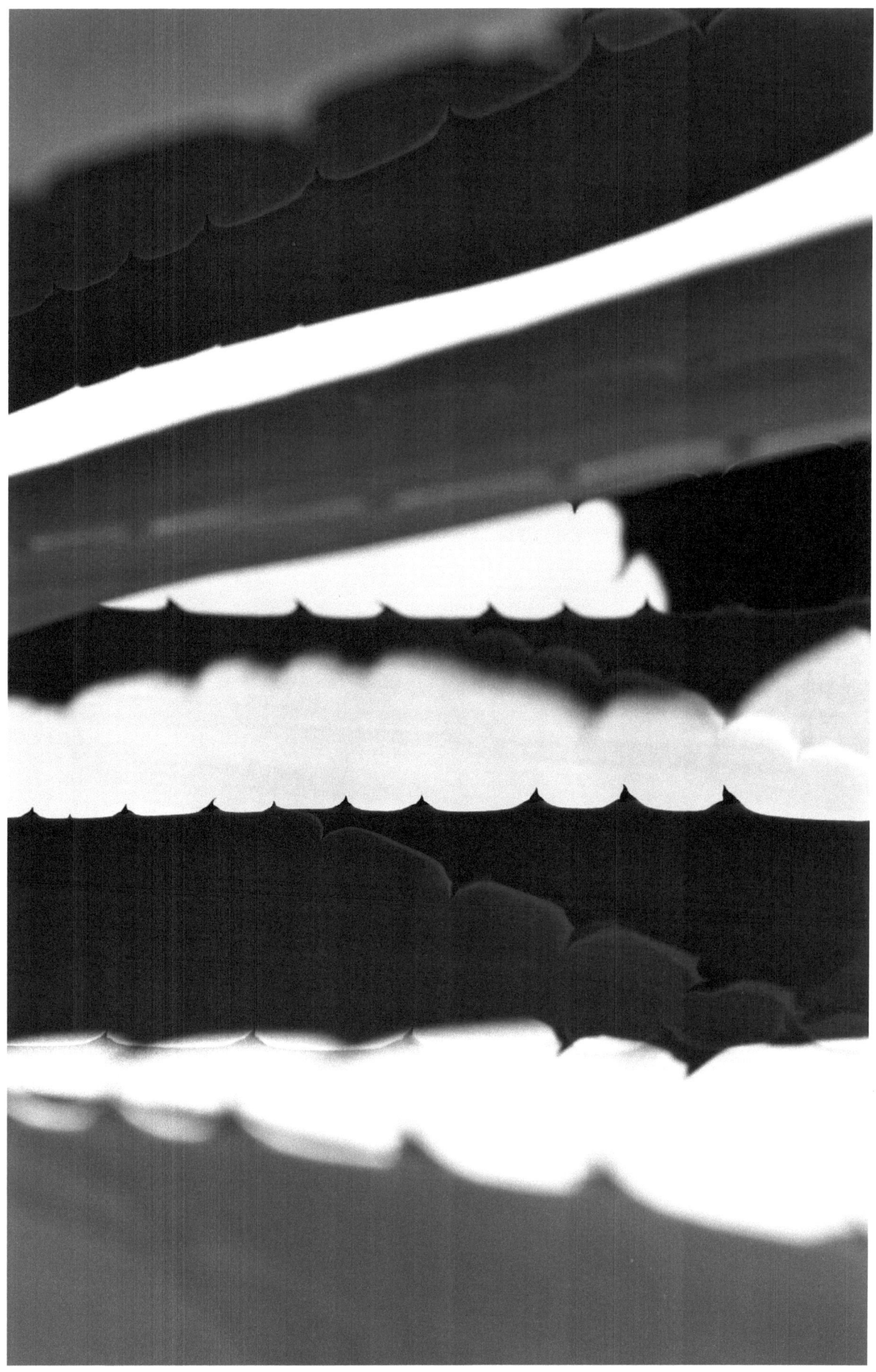

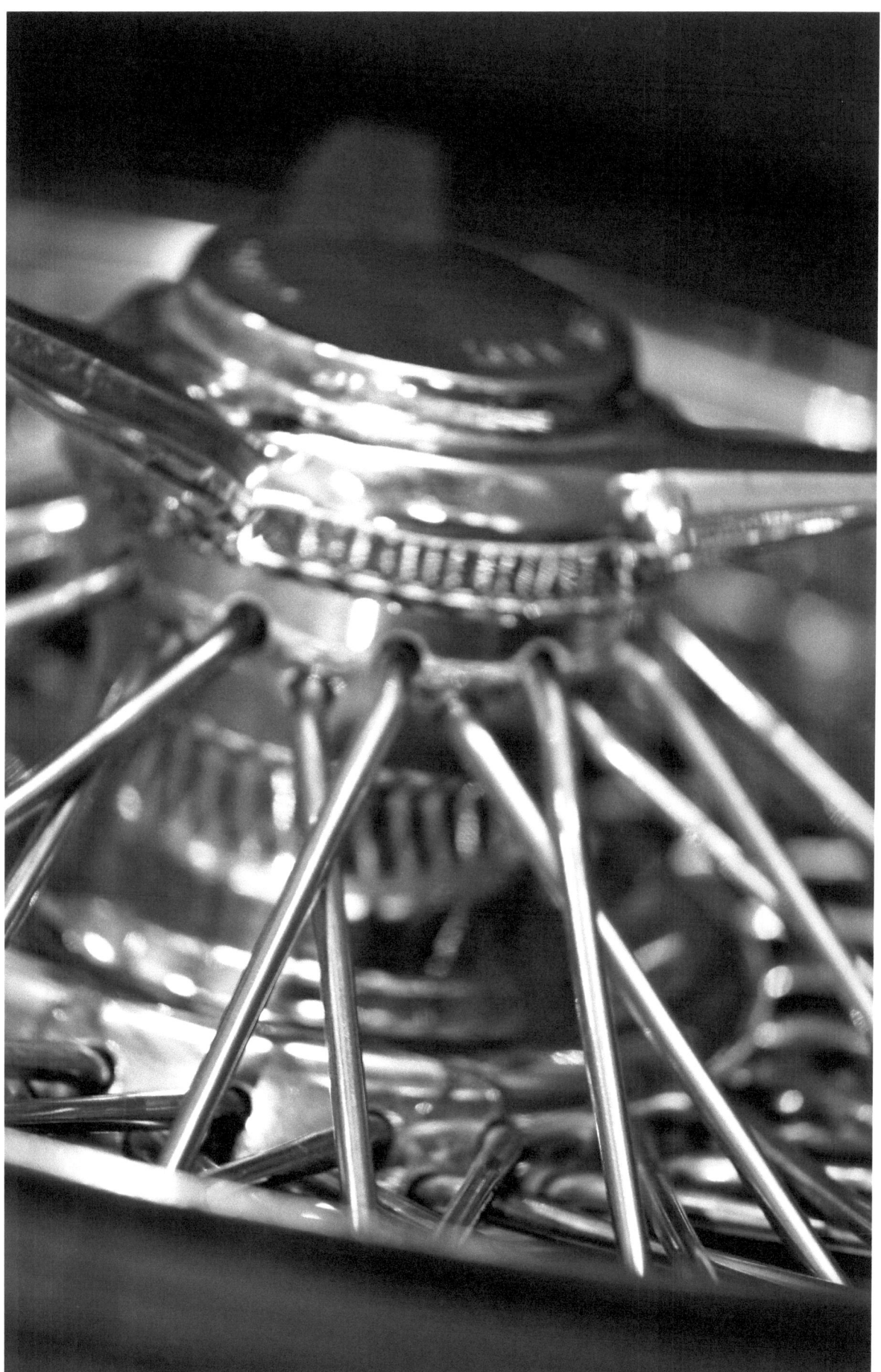

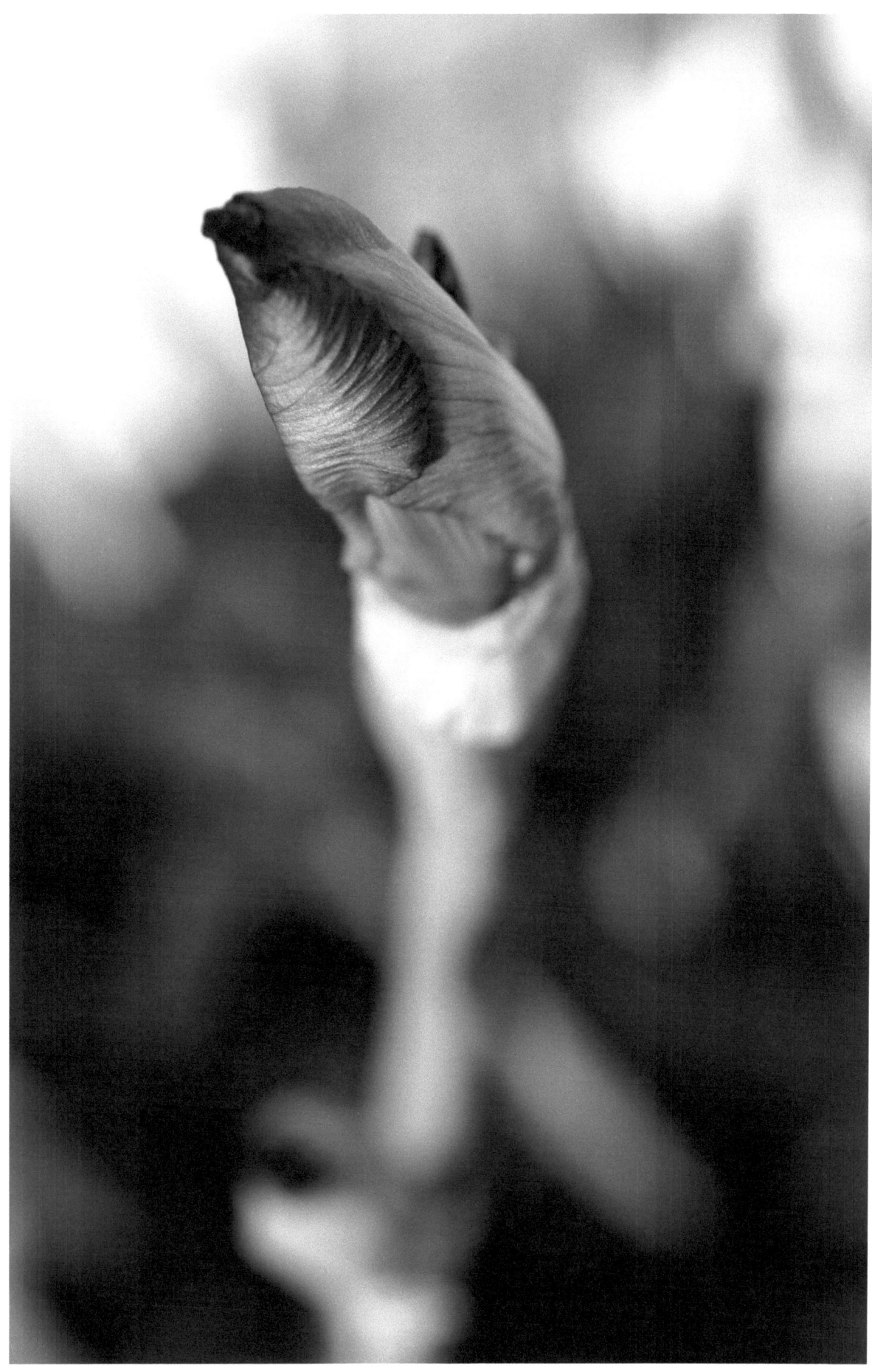

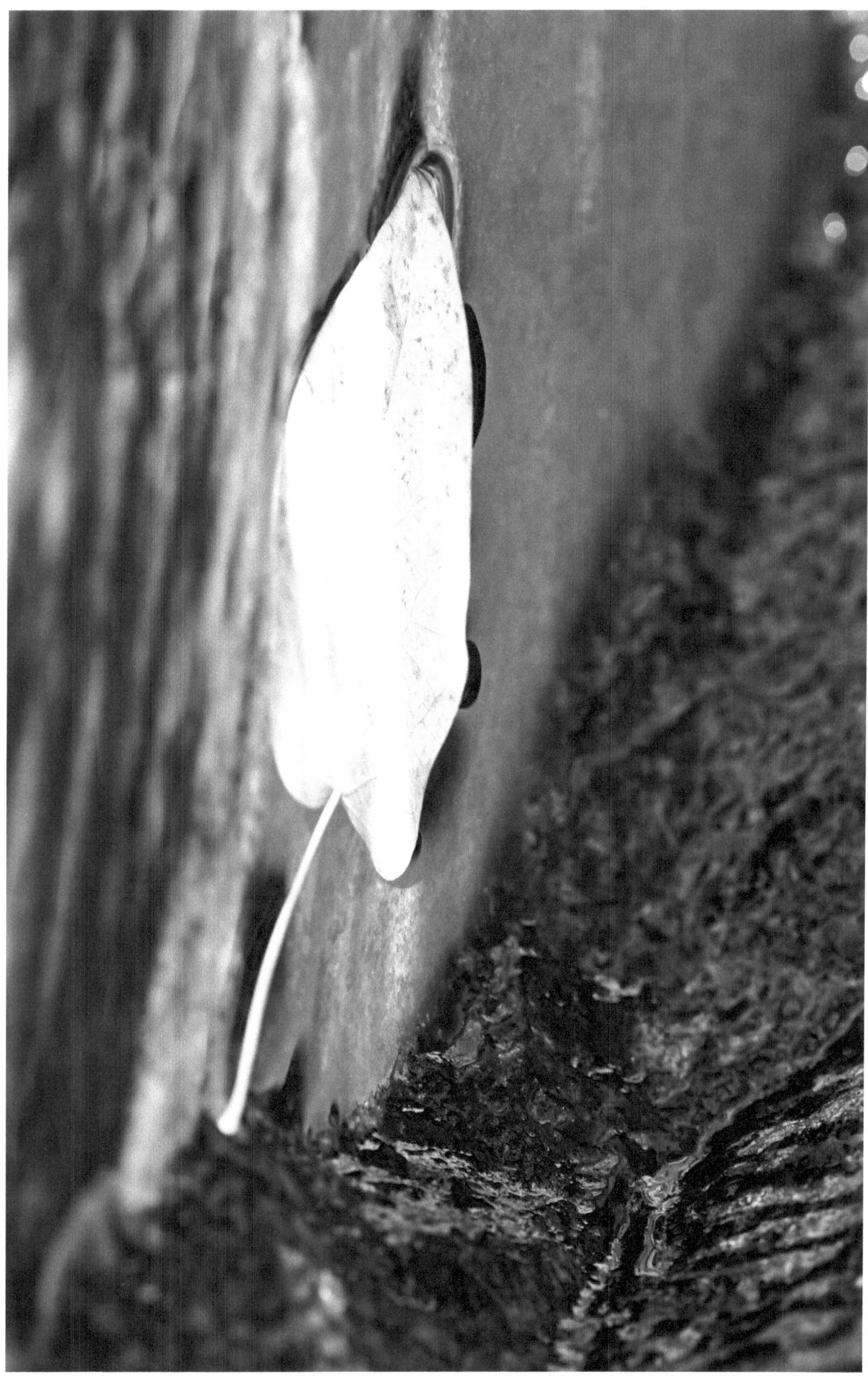

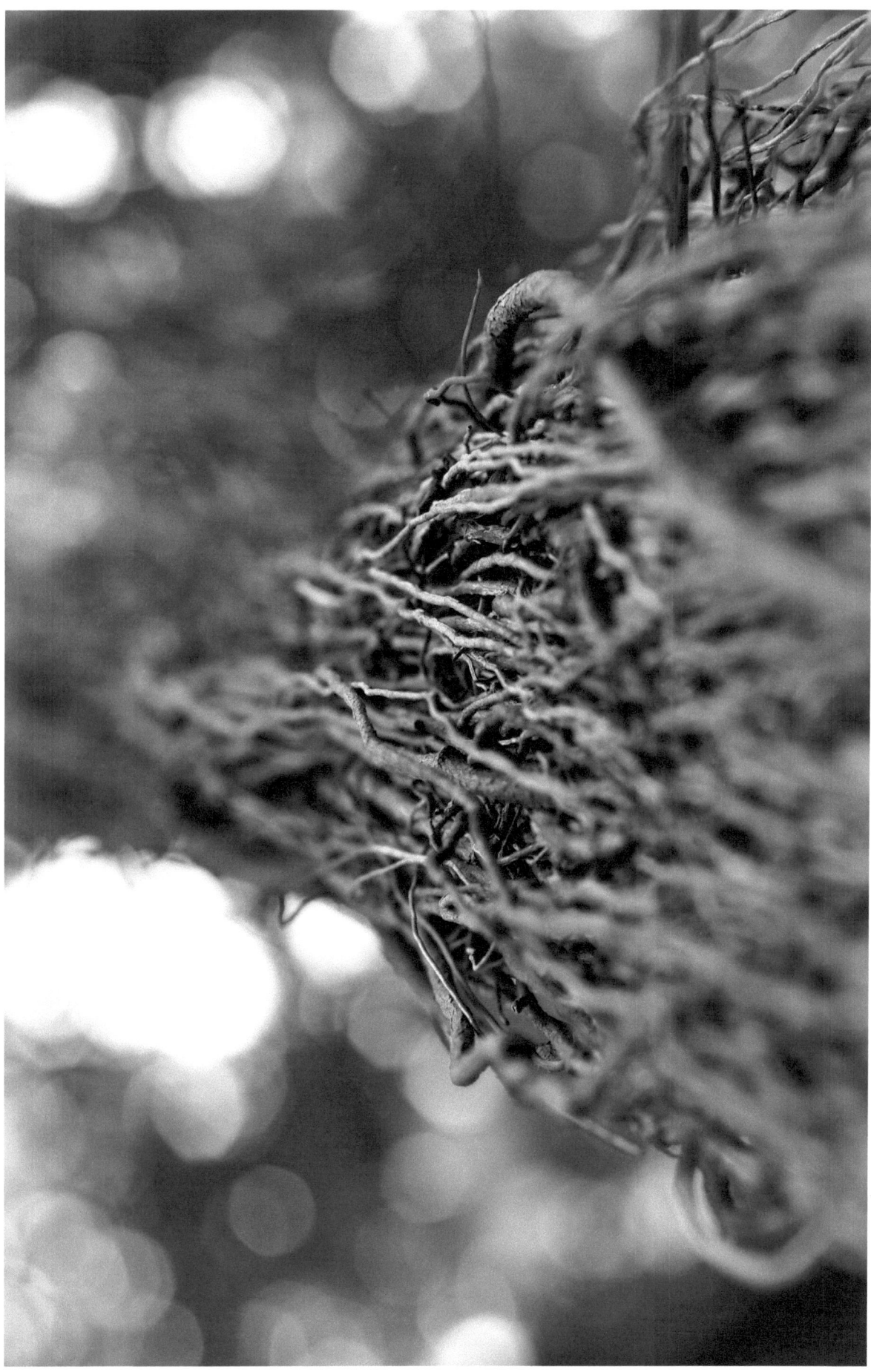

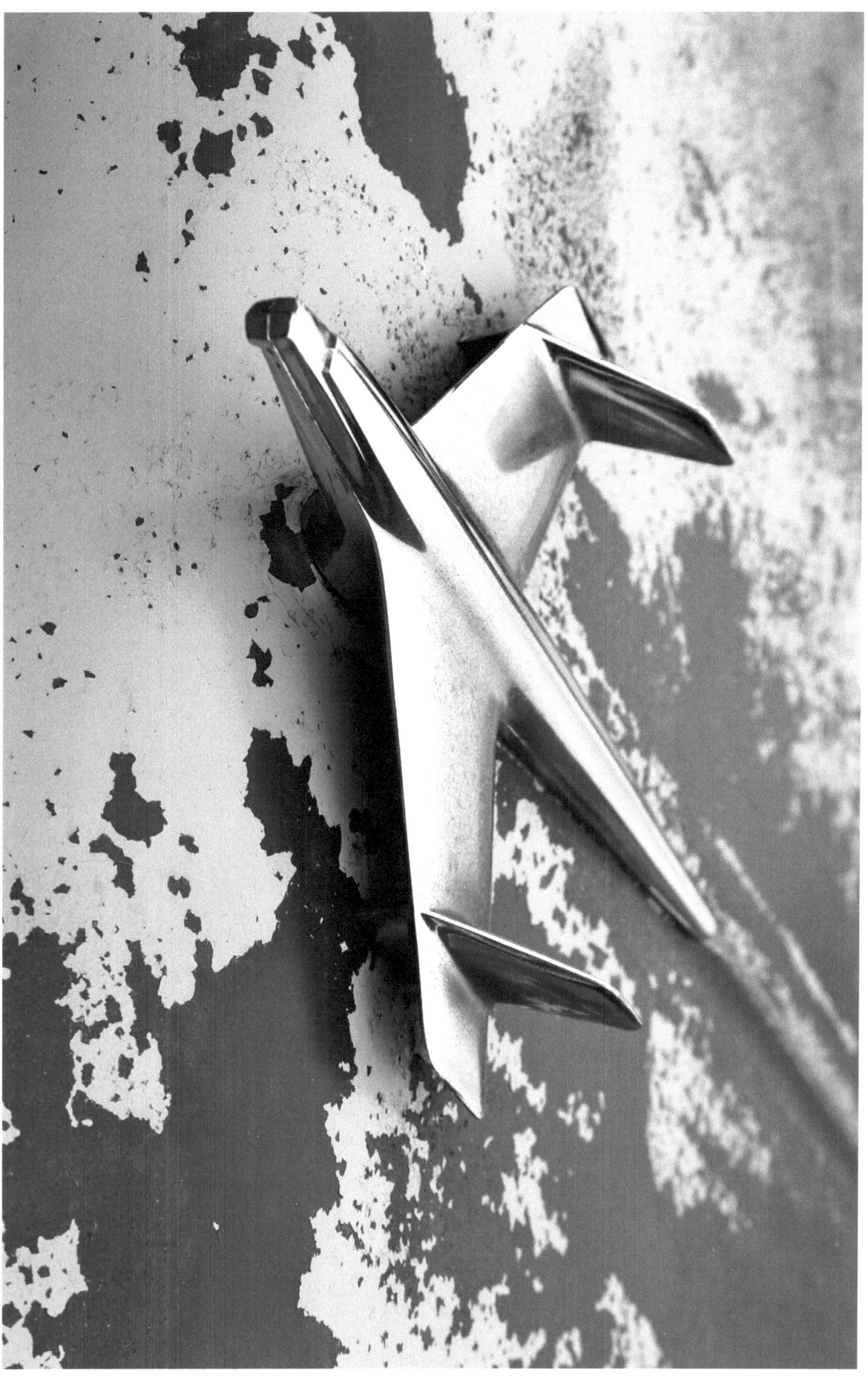

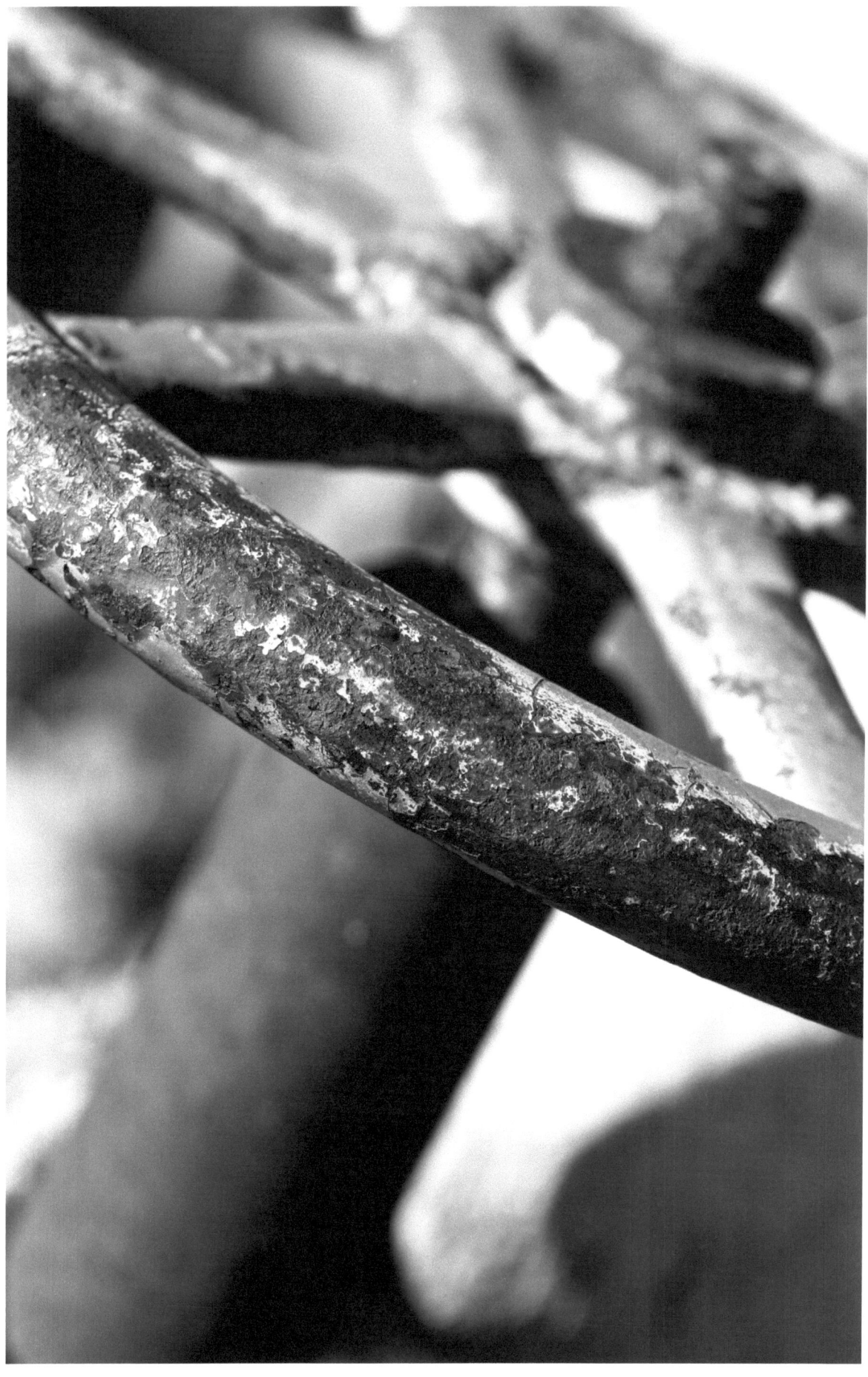

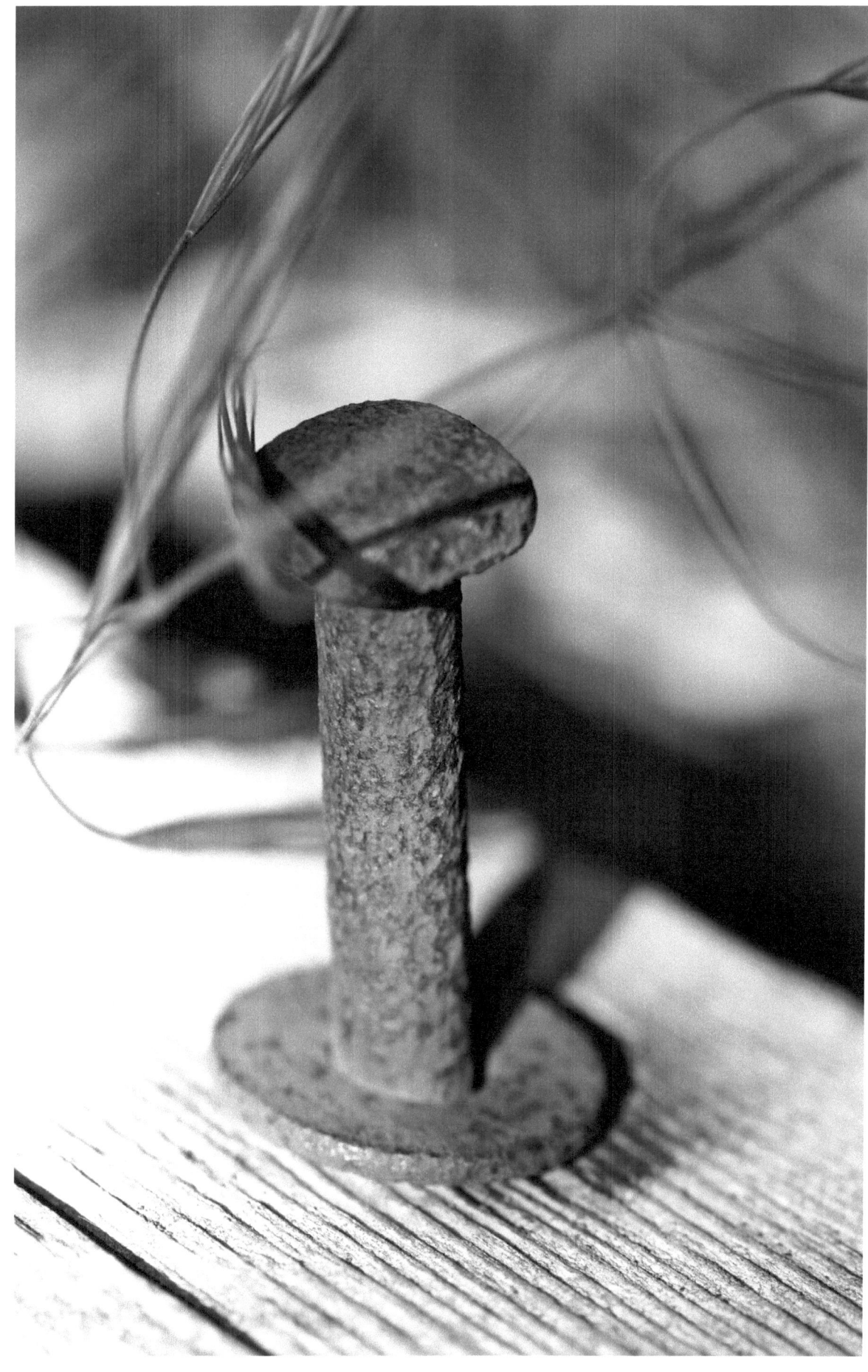

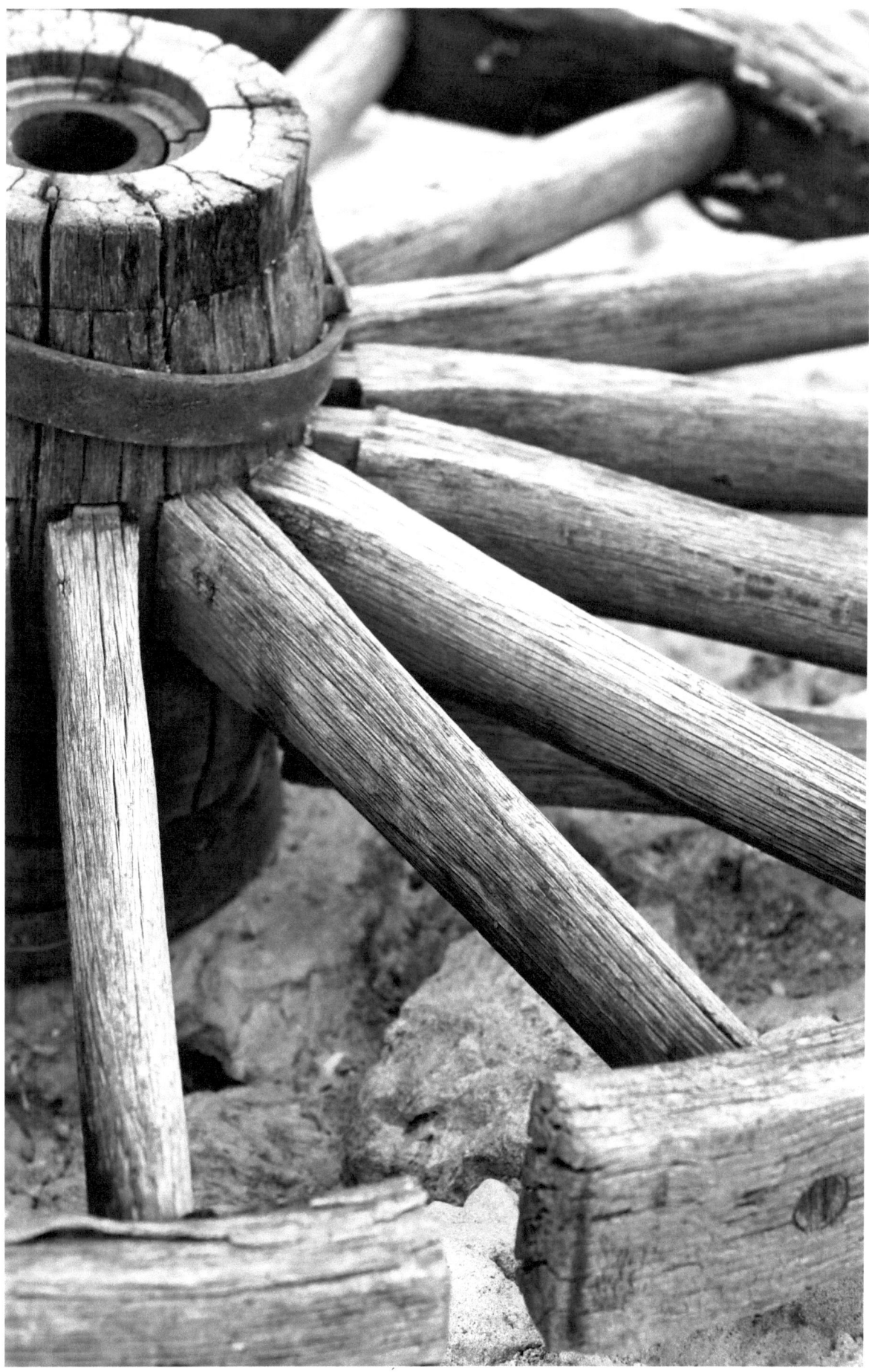

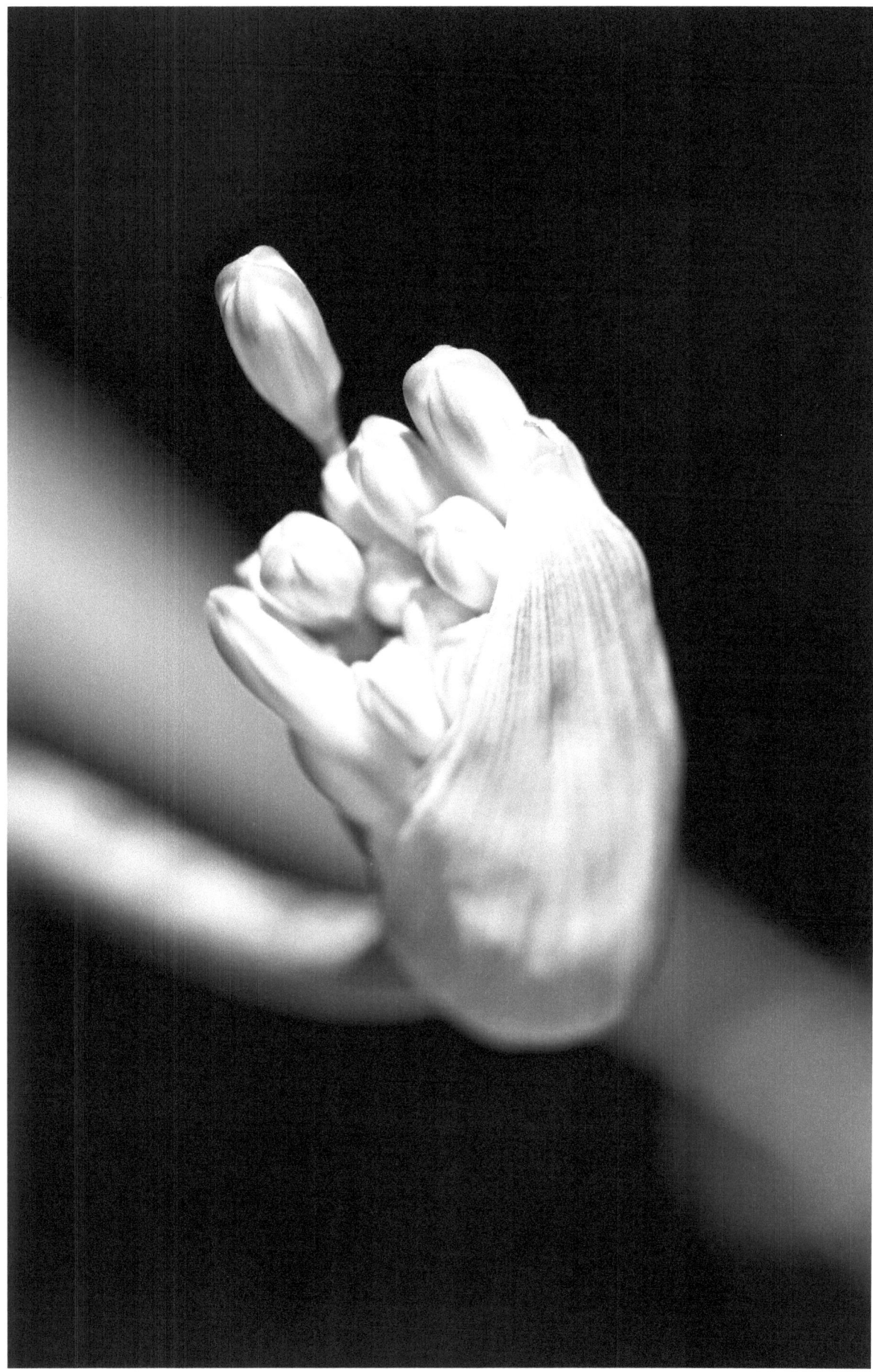

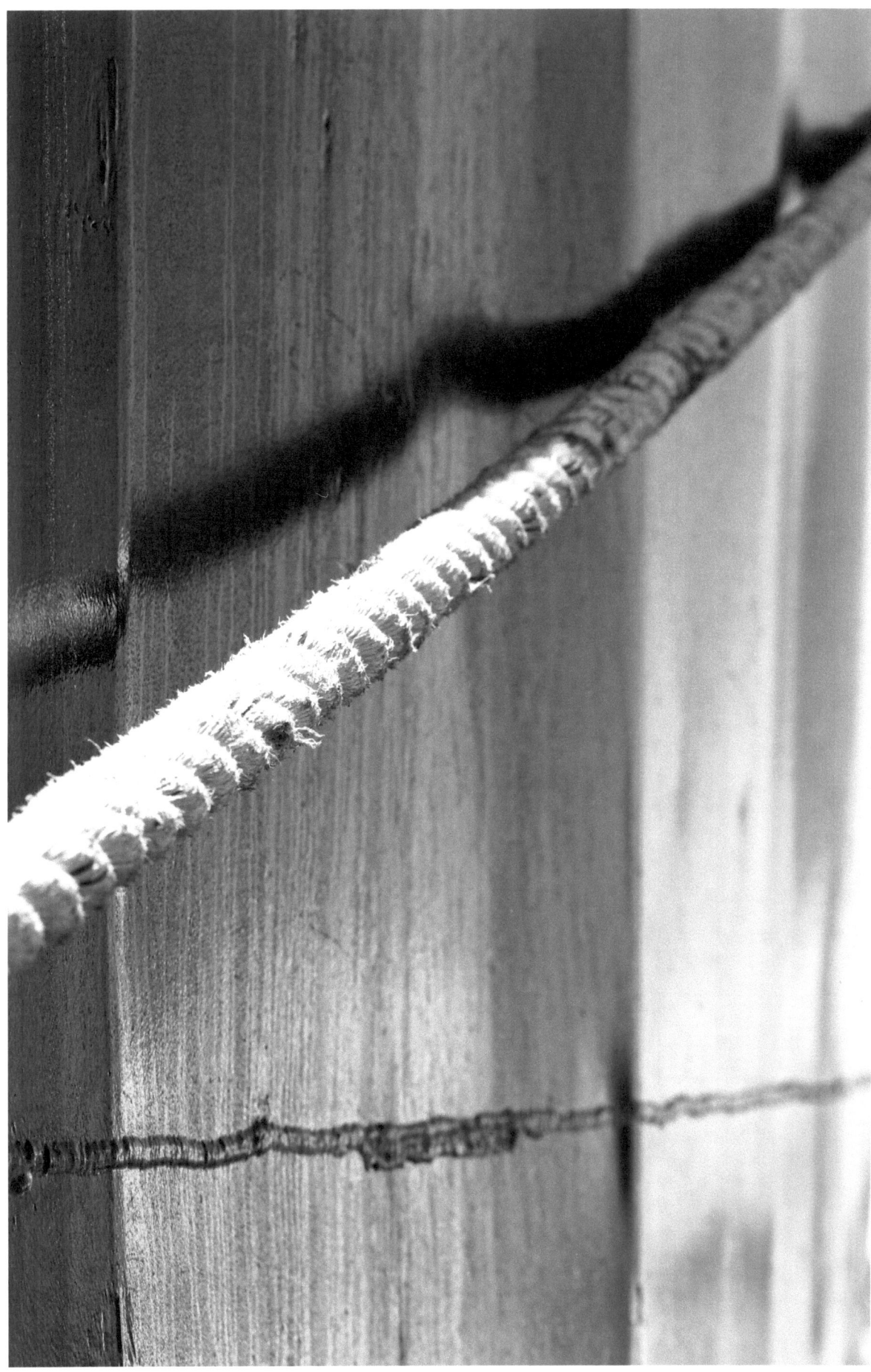

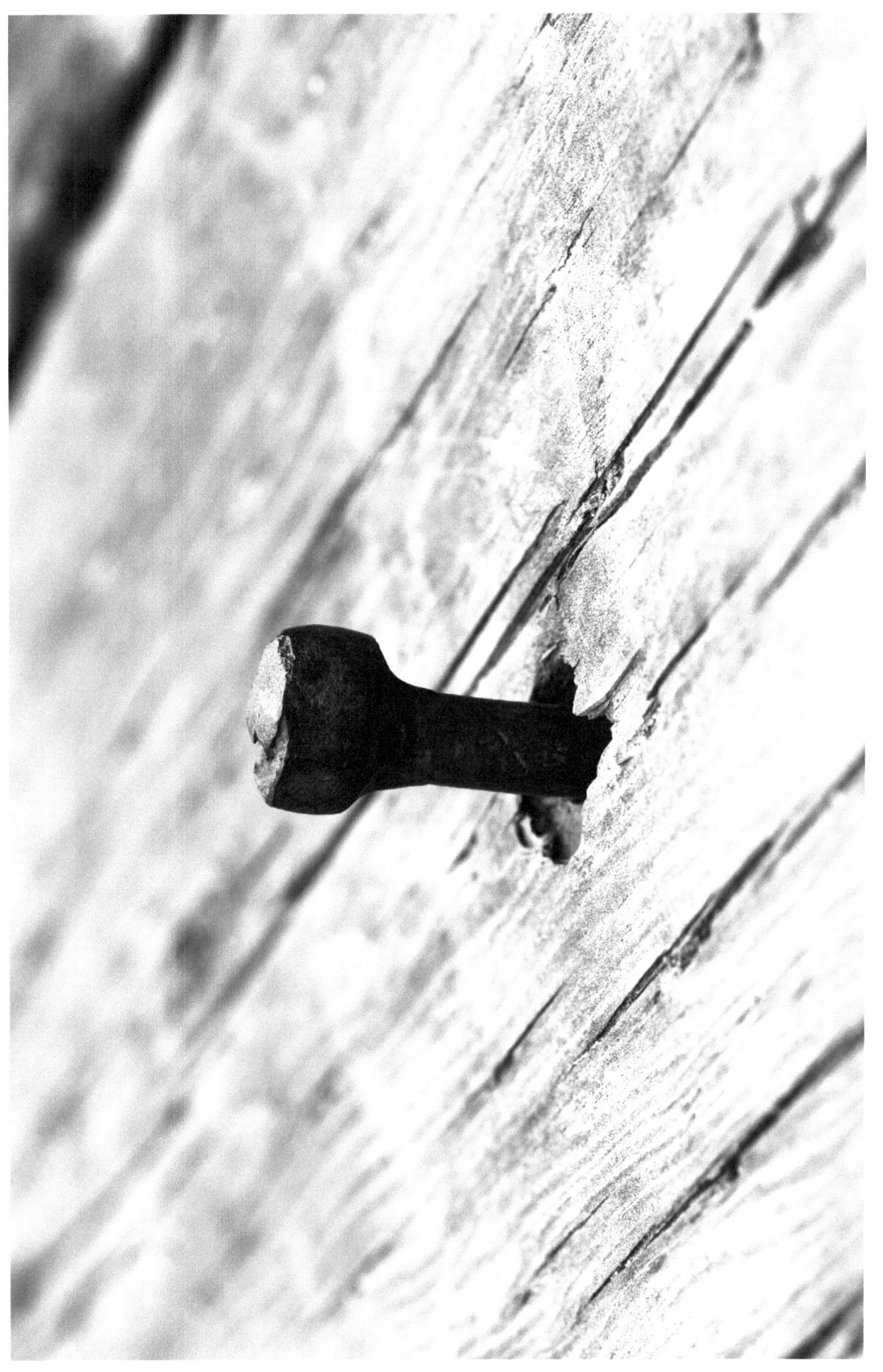

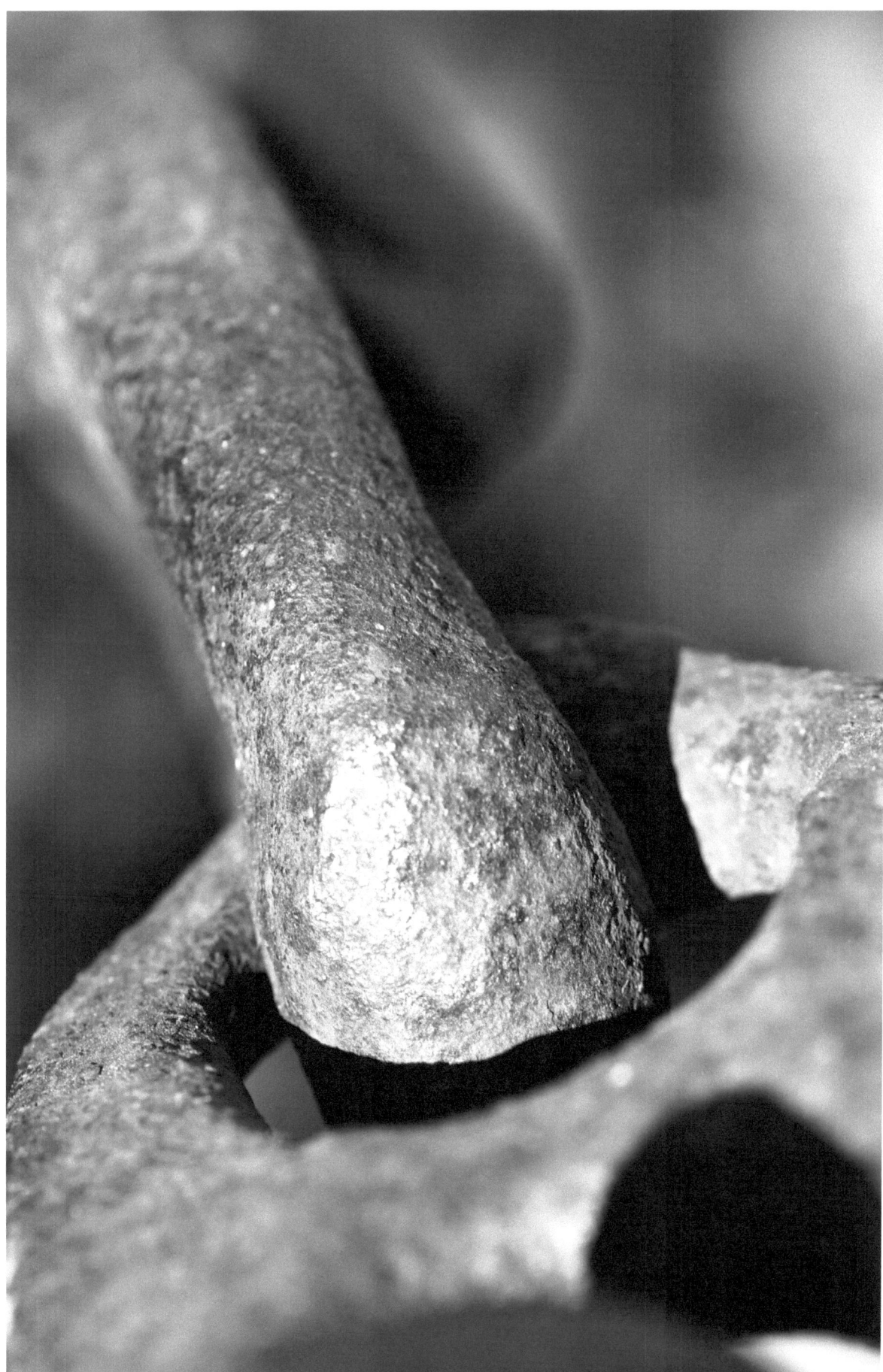

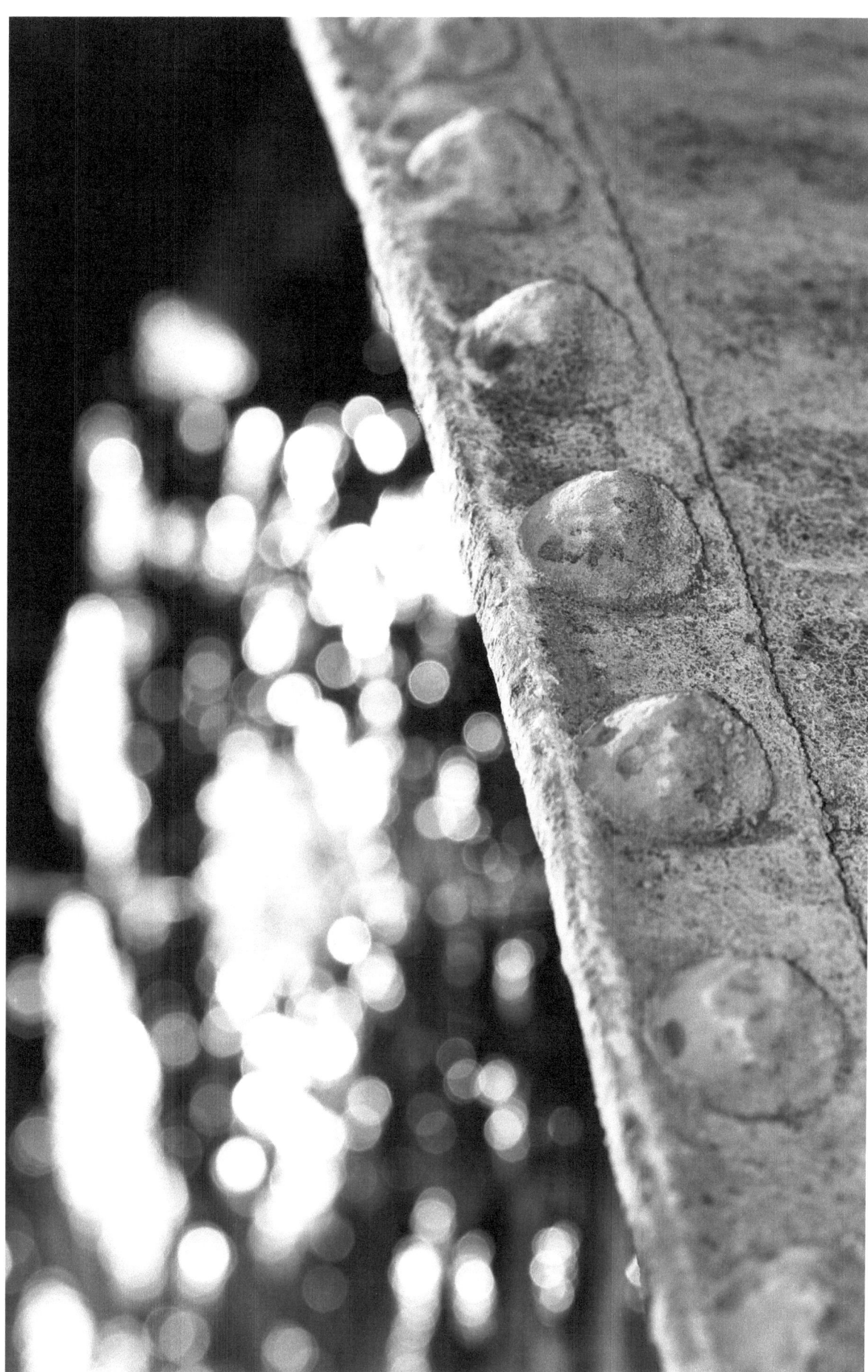

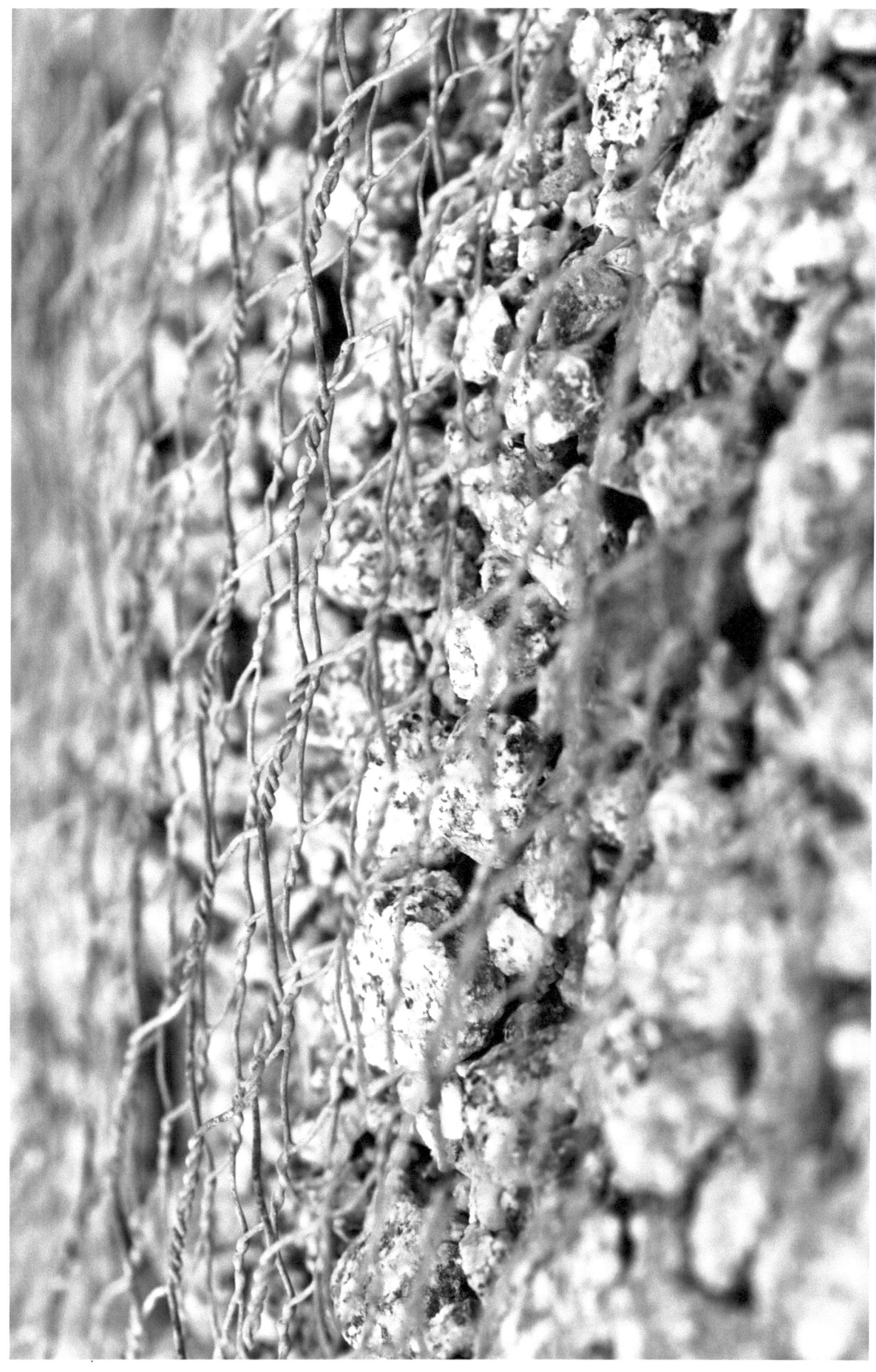

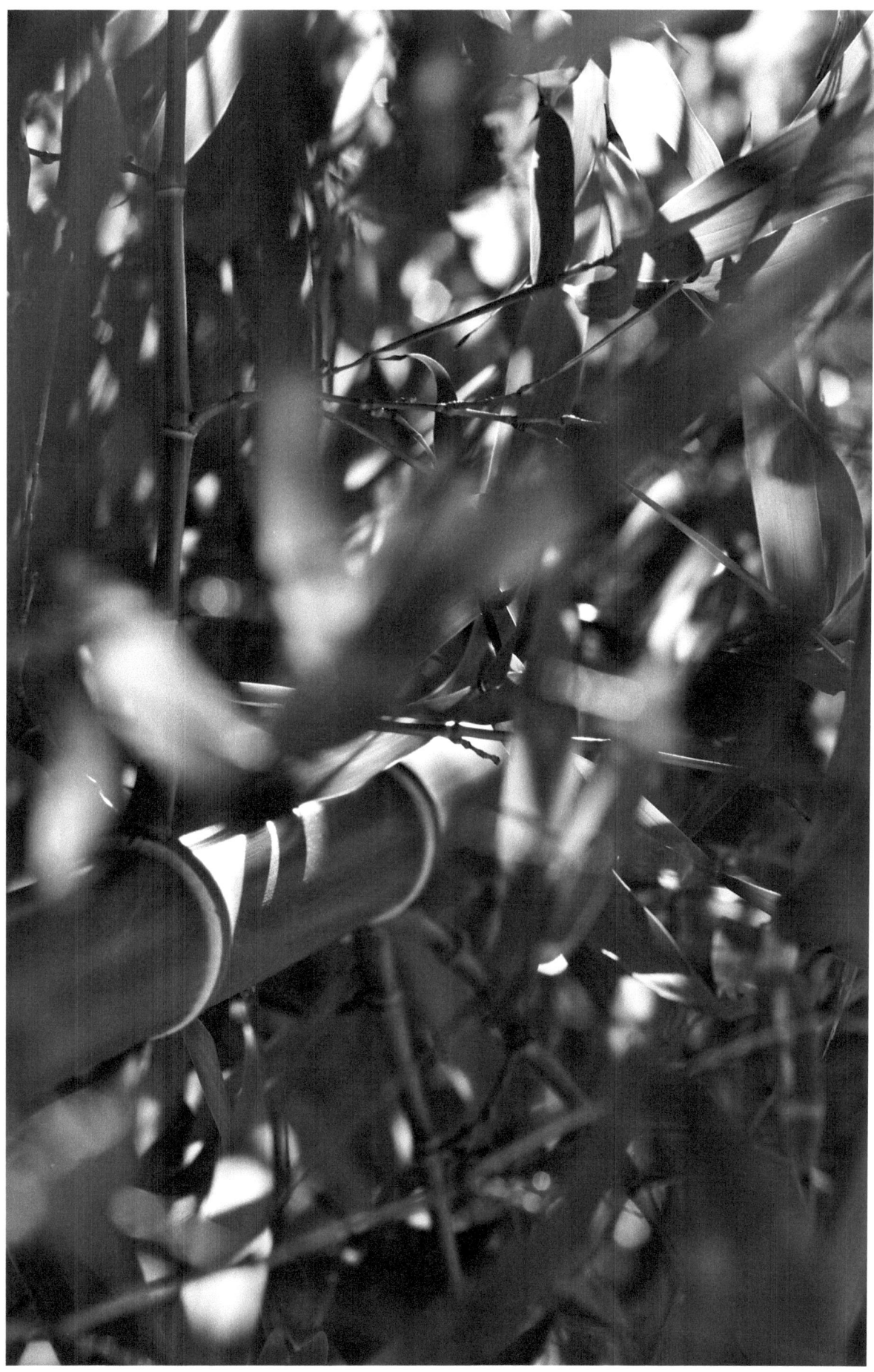

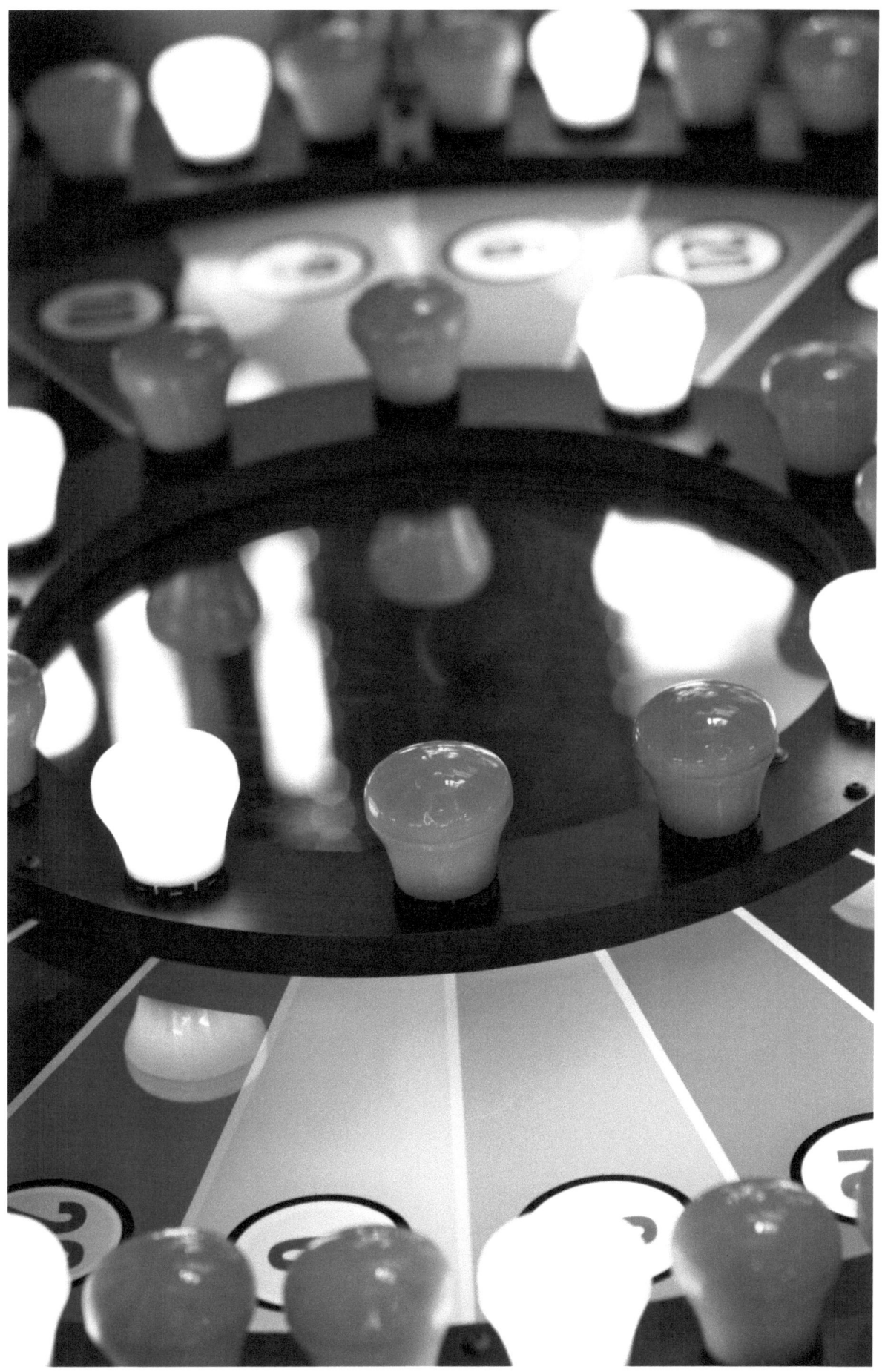

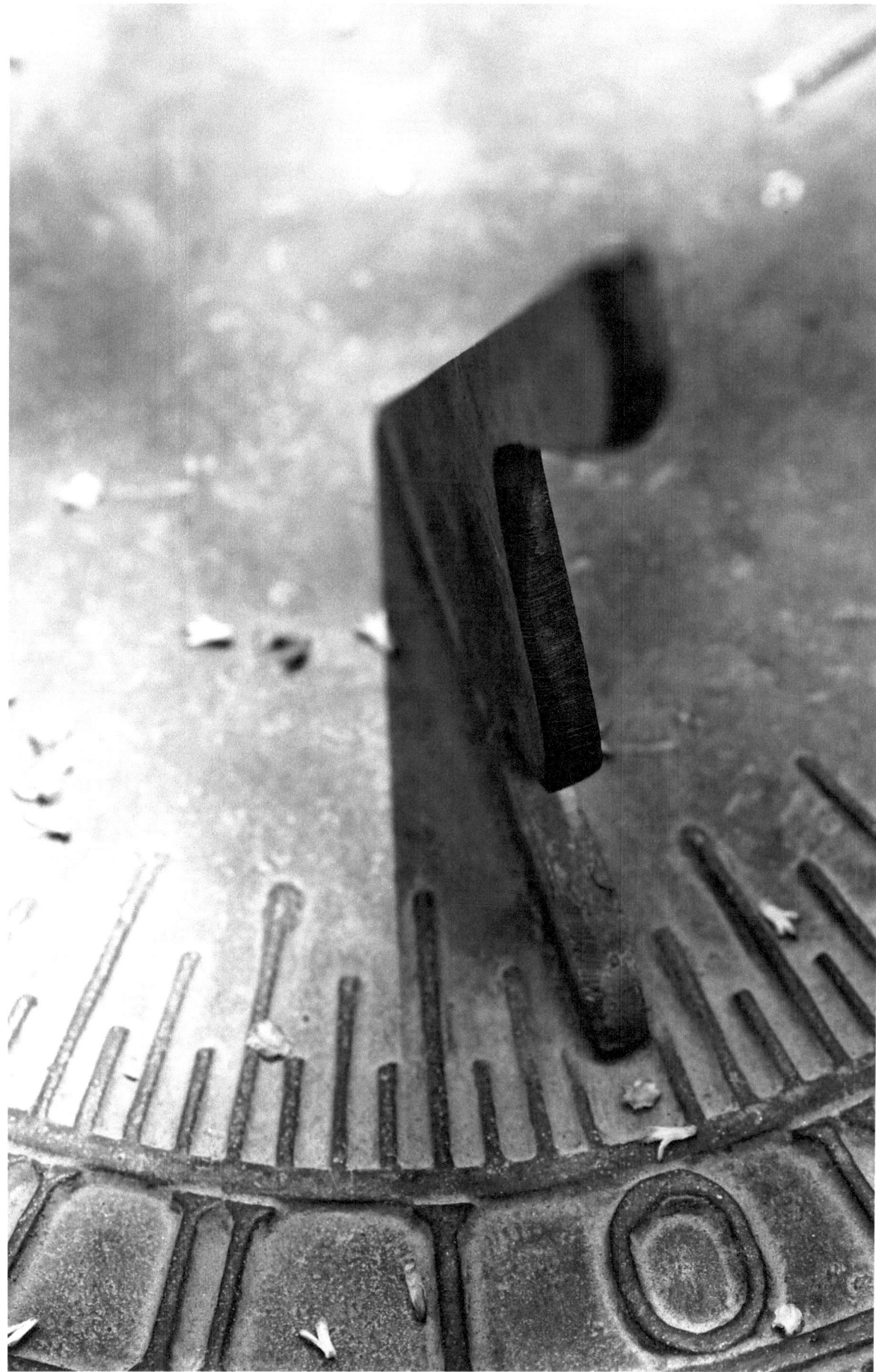